# A HALF-NAKED GEORGE WASHINGTON

## And Other True Tales From History

By
### RONALD G. SHAFER

*From The Washington Post Retropolis Column*
*Published 2024 in Williamsburg, Va. by Ronald G. Shafer*
*Retropolis columns with permission The Washington Post*
*Photos from the Library of Congress and the National Archives.*

Copyright © 2024 by Ronald G. Shafer
All rights reserved.

# TABLE OF CONTENTS

For my amazing wife, Mary Rogers,
In Williamsburg, Va.

*"History doesn't repeat itself, but it often rhymes."*

*– Mark Twain*

# INTRODUCTION

British Prime Minister Winston Churchill said those who fail to learn from history are doomed to repeat it. This is your chance to keep from being doomed. These articles tell the history behind some of today's news events. A former U.S. President once went on trial. Presidential papers were lost. The oldest man to run for president got elected. And, yes, Congress once removed a statue from inside the U.S. Capitol because it showed George Washington half naked. Shocking stuff.

I wrote most of these articles as a freelance writer for the Washington Post Retropolis column. My history is that I am a native of Columbus, Ohio, where I became the first Ohio State University journalism student ever hired by the Wall Street Journal. During 38 years at the Journal I was the Washington political features editor and writer of the page-one column the Washington Wire.

I now live in Williamsburg, Va., with my entrepreneur wife, Mary Rogers. I have written books about the start of the Brooklyn Dodgers ("When The Dodgers Were Bridegrooms"), the first modern presidential campaign ("The Carnival Campaign. How the Rollicking 1840 Campaign of Tippecanoe and Tyler Too Changed Presidential Elections Forever") and "Breaking News All Over Again," my first collection of Retropolis articles.

This new book follows an old rule: A brain-tickling way to learn about history is to read stories about history.

Ron Shafer

# SECTION 1:

# BAD OLD IDEAS

# CHAPTER 1

# A HALF-NAKED GEORGE WASHINGTON

By Ronald G. Shafer
*This article was first published in The Washington Post on Jan.22, 2023*

The first statue Congress voted to remove from the Capitol was one of George Washington — not because Washington was an enslaver like some others whose statues have been slated for removal, but because the statue was scandalous. The first president was portrayed naked to the waist in a toga with his right finger pointing toward the sky and his left hand clasping a sheathed sword.

"The man does not live, and never lived, who saw Washington without his shirt," complained Rep. Henry Wise, a Virginia Whig.

Of the thousands of statues of Washington, this one, by American sculptor Horatio Greenough, is the most controversial. To mark Washington's 100th birthday, in 1832 Congress authorized the creation of what it expected to be a reverent rendition of the United States' most revered founder. President Andrew Jackson picked the 27-year-old Greenough for the task, and Greenough labored on his creation in Italy for more than eight years. When his 12-ton marble statue was squeezed into the Capitol Rotunda in late 1841, during the presidency of John Tyler, many onlookers were aghast.

FIGURE 1: GEORGE WASHINGTON STATUE OUTSIDE CAPITOL

The 12-foot-high statue showed Washington's head atop a very buff and bare-chested body, resembling a Greek or Roman god. He sat on a chair wearing sandals and a toga, part of which was draped over his bent right arm.

"I fear this statue will only give the idea of entering or leaving a bath," said Charles Bulfinch, the former architect of the Capitol. He added that the statue should be sent to Athens "to be placed in the Parthenon with other naked great men." Former New York mayor Philip Hone wrote in his diary that the statue looked "like a great herculean Warrior — like Venus of the Bath — undraped, with a huge napkin lying on his lap." Sen. William Preston, a South Carolina Whig, called the statue "the most horrid phantasmagoria I have ever beheld."

People were shocked to see the great general in the buff. "Did you ever see Washington naked?" author Nathaniel Hawthorne wrote, tongue in cheek. "It is inconceivable. He had nakedness, but I imagine was born with his clothes on and his hair powdered and made a stately bow on his first appearance in the world." When British author Charles Dickens visited the statue in 1842, he wrote, "It has great merit, of course, but it struck me as being rather strained and violent for its subject."

Not everybody hated the statue. Essayist Ralph Waldo Emerson described it as "simple & grand, nobly draped below & nobler nude above." Emerson agreed with

Greenough that the problem was the poor lighting in the Rotunda, especially with the statue perched atop a 13-foot wooden platform. On Jan. 11, 1843, the two men made a nighttime visit to view the colossal statue by torchlight. It did not go well.

"Higher, higher," Greenough shouted to the lamp holder, according to House historians, who wrote, "Soon, flames leapt from the lamps to the wooden box and pole that held them aloft." The box, Emerson wrote a friend, was "let down rapidly, lamps melting & exploding & brilliant balls of light falling on the floor." The two men dragged the "brilliant bonfire" safely outdoors, he wrote.

Greenough lobbied for the statue to be moved elsewhere at the Capitol, and Congress was happy to oblige. Wise argued for dumping most of the monument altogether. "The head, he said, was a good one; he would have that sawed off and placed in a suitable position," the New York Evening Post reported, "but he would tumble the body of the statue into the Potomac." Rep. John Quincy Adams, a Massachusetts Whig and former president, voted to move the statue "for the reason that water dripped down on it" from the roof, the Congressional Globe reported.

In 1843, Congress had the statue moved outside to the Capitol's East Plaza and placed on a granite pedestal engraved with the words, "First in war, first in peace and first in the hearts of his countrymen." The move brought the statue's total cost to the equivalent of $1.2 million today. "Had I been ordered to make a statue for any square or similar situation at this metropolis," Greenough complained, "I should have represented Washington on horseback and in his actual dress."

The sculptor continued to defend his work as a symbol of liberty. While "my statue was the butt of wiseacres and witlings, I never in word, or thought, swerved from my principle," he wrote. He predicted in time it would be judged a great work of art. He was wrong.

The statue drew even more ridicule on public display outside the Capitol. Pranksters put top hats on Washington's head and cigars in his lips, and children playfully sat in his lap.

Meanwhile, some of the first president's clothes were put on display in a nearby Patent Office museum. A standing joke was that if Washington's statue could talk, the great man would say, "Here is my sword; my clothes are at the Patent Office."

In the early 1900s, The Washington Post mounted an editorial campaign urging Congress to move the statue again. The statue, The Post wrote, portrays Washington "in garb in which he could not have appeared at any stage of his career" without making people think "he had become insane and needed the restraints of a lunatic asylum." In 1908, Congress voted to move the statue inside the "nation's attic," the Smithsonian Institution castle on the National Mall.

In November 1908, "George Washington, dismantled, disfigured and clad in a marble toga, and temporarily disgraced, was hauled through the streets of the

National Capital today, unattended by an honorary escort save a dozen or more laborers who had taken a professional delight in driving George from the Capitol Grounds," the Washington Times reported.

The Washington Star printed a pretend interview with Washington from Mount Vernon. "Whoever heard of a first American making such a blooming fool of himself as to sit up on a cracker barrel with a towel over one shoulder and nothing else on but a pair of things they called sandals and holding on to a toy sword with one hand?" this Washington said. "Even at Valley Forge I had more clothes than that. And I was down to my last uniform, too."

FIGURE 2: WASHINGTON AT NATIONAL MUSEUM OF AMERICAN HISTORY

The statue sat in a dusty corner until 1964, when it was moved to the Smithsonian's new Museum of History and Technology (now the National Museum of American History), where it still got negative reviews. The New York Daily News, under the headline "It Was a Big Flop The First Time Out," wrote: "What's needed now is another petition to put George the Greek back in the attic."

Today, the half-naked Washington sits on the museum's second floor, seeming to greet visitors with a wave.

# CHAPTER 2

# NAMING A FORT AFTER A
# TERRIBLE GENERAL

By Ronald G. Shafer
*This article was first published in The Washington Post on June 16, 2023*

The enslaving Confederate Gen. Braxton Bragg suddenly has become a Republican rallying cry, after Fort Bragg in North Carolina was renamed to Fort Liberty.

"We will end the political correctness in the hallways of the Pentagon, and North Carolina will once again be home to Fort Bragg," former vice president Mike Pence told a state GOP convention. "It's an iconic name and iconic base, and we're not gonna let political correctness run amok in North Carolina," vowed Florida Gov. Ron DeSantis.

Fort Bragg does have a venerable military history, of course. But its eponym, Gen. Bragg, not so much. Bragg was a "merciless tyrant" who had an "uncanny ability to turn minor wins and losses into strategic defeat," wrote Sam Watkins, who served under the man historians call the South's worst and most hated general.

Bragg, a U.S. Military Academy graduate from North Carolina, first gained fame in the Mexican American War when artillery troops fired armed projectiles called "grape shots." During the 1847 Battle of Buena Vista, Gen. Zachary Taylor rode his horse over to Bragg and supposedly said, "Give them a little more grape, Captain Bragg." The phrase, a variation of the actual order, became so famous that Taylor used it in his successful 1848 presidential campaign.

But as a company commander, Bragg became known for his ruthless style that didn't exactly endear him to his troops, such as the time he ordered a soldier to ride into enemy fire to retrieve harnesses from dead artillery horses. One soldier tried to kill Bragg, slipping a 12-pound artillery shell under Bragg's cot; the shell exploded, destroying the cot, but Bragg was uninjured.

FIGURE 3: GEN. BRAXTON BRAGG

When the Civil War broke out, Confederate President Jefferson Davis called on Bragg to leave his Louisiana sugar plantation and 105 people he enslaved to be a rebel officer. In his first campaign as a full general, in 1862, Bragg brashly invaded Kentucky, figuring he would be welcomed with open arms. He issued a proclamation: "Kentuckians! I have entered your State with the Confederate Army of the West and offer you an opportunity to free yourselves from the tyranny of a despotic ruler" — meaning President Abraham Lincoln.

Bragg's "insufferable piece of nonsense," the Louisville Courier responded, "reminds us very much of the song, 'Will you walk into my parlor, said the spider to the fly.'" Most Kentuckians didn't rally to Bragg's call, and he retreated by year's end.

The day after Christmas, Bragg directed a firing squad to execute a 19-year-old infantryman, Asa Lewis, who had been convicted of desertion after going to the Kentucky home of his widowed mother without permission. When Confederate

Gen John Breckinridge of Kentucky appealed for mercy, Bragg sneered: "You Kentuckians are too independent for the good of the army. I'll shoot every one of them if I have to." Lewis's execution proceeded.

Bragg led his troops the next year into Tennessee, where he suffered a string of losses, leaving Union troops in control of Middle Tennessee. In September, he finally scored a win at the bloody Battle of Chickamauga, in northern Georgia, but fellow officers, including Gen. Nathan Bedford Forrest, berated him for not pursuing the Union troops to stop them from retreating to nearby Chattanooga, Tenn.

After a personal clash with Bragg, Forrest burst into Bragg's tent and shouted, "You have played the part of a damned scoundrel, and are a coward, and if you were any part of a man, I would slap your jaws ... If you ever again try to interfere with me or cross my path, it will be at the peril of your life," according to John Wyeth's 1899 biography of Forrest.

Bragg's subordinate officers were so upset with the general's decisions that 12 of them signed and sent a secret petition to Davis urging him to replace Bragg. Davis traveled to the battle site to talk to Bragg but decided to keep him. Bragg's failure to destroy the fleeing Union army, though, came back to bite him. Gen. Ulysses S. Grant took command of the Union forces, which in late November proceeded to trounce Bragg's in the Chattanooga campaign.

Following his humiliating defeat, Bragg offered his resignation to Davis, who accepted it and made the general a military adviser in Richmond. After the war, Bragg worked as a civil engineer in Alabama and Texas, but he left both positions after getting into arguments with his bosses. He died in 1876, at age 59.

The general faded into history thereafter until World War I, when Major Gen. William J. Snow, the Army's chief of field artillery, began looking for locations to build two new artillery training camps. He settled on one area in Kentucky and another in North Carolina, near Fayetteville. Snow also was in charge of Camp Zachary Taylor in Kentucky. "The name was so long, and it irritated me to take so much time in frequently writing or speaking about it," the general wrote in his 1941 memoir.

So he decided to name the two new camps after past artillery officers with short names. He named the Kentucky camp, now Fort Knox, after Henry Knox, chief artillery officer in the American Revolutionary War and the first U.S. war secretary. He named the other camp after Bragg, a North Carolina native.

Bragg's biographers refer to his racism, with Earl J. Hess noting that Bragg opposed drafting enslaved people into the Confederate army because "he did not believe they could be made into reliable soldiers." Such a view might have been no problem to Snow, who in his own book said he refused to accept Black draftees into artillery units because "I could not make field artillerymen of them."

Camp Bragg opened in 1918 and was upgraded to Fort Bragg in 1922. The post was one of nine Southern Army bases named after Confederate leaders being renamed after the 2020 killing of George Floyd. The other bases are being named after individual heroes and heroines, but the Fort Bragg naming committee pressed for the name Liberty as symbolizing the post's mission.

That's a far cry from the image of the fort's original eponym. "Bragg," Confederate officer William Dudley Hale wrote in a letter after the war, "was obstinate but without firmness, ruthless without enterprise, crafty yet without stratagem, suspicious, envious, jealous, vain, a bantam in success and a dunghill in disaster."

# CHAPTER 3

# LETTING A SUPREME COURT JUSTICE PICK A PRESIDENT

By Ronald G. Shafer.
*This article was first published in The Washington Post on April 25, 2024.*

Supreme Court Justice Joseph P. Bradley isn't exactly a household name, but no justice has played a more high-profile role in presidential politics. After the 1876 election, newspapers labeled him "Joe Bradley, our President maker."

As the Supreme Court hears arguments on whether former president Donald Trump is immune from prosecution, the justices are under scrutiny for any role they may play in the outcome of the 2024 presidential election. But long before the court's messy involvement in this year's race or its one-vote majority that put George W. Bush in the White House in 2000, Bradley was the decider in the razor-close contest between Republican Rutherford B. Hayes of Ohio and Democrat Samuel Tilden of New York. The justice became the poster boy — and, to many Democrats, the villain — on a commission created by Congress to resolve one of America's most convoluted presidential elections ever.

FIGURE 4: SUPREME COURT JUSTICE JOSEPH P. BRADLEY

The outcome was still up in the air on Jan. 29, 1877, nearly 12 weeks after the election, with Tilden one short of the 185 electoral votes needed. Twenty electoral votes were still unresolved because of competing submissions from South Carolina, Louisiana and Florida — where White Democrats had attacked Black Republican voters, prompting charges of interference — and from Oregon, where one electoral vote was disputed.

Nobody knew it at the time, but the process for deciding the election would end up destroying the rights of Black people in the South. For now, the focus was on picking a president before the March 5 inauguration.

So Congress created a 15-member electoral commission, consisting of five senators, five House members and five Supreme Court justices. The members were split evenly between Republicans and Democrats, plus Justice David Davis, a political independent. But then Davis, of Illinois, resigned to accept an appointment to the U.S. Senate as a Democrat.

To replace him, the commission turned to Bradley, a moderate Republican appointed by outgoing President Ulysses S. Grant, as the least partisan of the remaining justices. The 63-year-old Bradley, a former farm boy who became a wealthy New Jersey railroad lawyer, would be the potential tiebreaker.

Bradley was a "cold man" who "convinces by the force of his argument rather than captures by the brilliancy of his rhetoric," the New York Herald wrote. "His mind is eminently judicial."

The panel began public hearings on Feb. 1 in the Supreme Court room at the Capitol. (The court didn't get its own building until 1935.) Justices on the commission didn't dress in their usual black robes and "look odd without their gowns," the New York Times observed.

Florida's four electoral votes were the first up for debate. Bradley allegedly planned to back the legitimacy of the Democratic electors, making Tilden president, a Democratic congressman from New Jersey later alleged, but changed his mind at home that night under pressure from Republican friends. Bradley denied those claims. His vote created an 8-7 majority to accept Florida's electors for Hayes.

Next up was Louisiana, and all eyes were on Bradley. "He is generally regarded as the man on who the whole thing turns," the Louisville Courier Journal wrote. The justice again led an 8-7 vote for the eight Hayes electors, augmenting Democratic doubts about his objectivity.

"It is very funny to see the old New Jersey man sitting in the Tribunal with seven Democrats on one side" and "humming abstractly that well-known air, 'Ho, waltz to Joseph if you please; he will never waltz with you—' which is the situation in a nutshell," the New Orleans Democrat wrote.

Sure enough, Bradley joined the 8-7 majority to award Hayes one disputed electoral vote in Oregon and seven in South Carolina, effectively electing Hayes president unless Congress rejected the results.

Furious Democrats focused their anger on the head of the vile "Bradley Tribunal." Democratic newspapers sprinkled their pages with epithets about the justice: "The American Judas-Bradley." "The umpire who stole a Presidency." "Captain Kidd would have been a better man than Bradley in his place.

The New York Sun wrote that the Washington Monument should be torn down and the stones piled up again, and "at the top of all put a colossal statue of Joe Bradley, the President-maker," with "his hand stretched out toward the White House."

"Somebody tied crape to the doorknob of perjured Bradley's residence in Washington, and with it a slip on which was written, 'Justice is dead,'" the San Francisco Examiner reported.

"The abuse heaped upon me" is "almost beyond conception," Bradley wrote. His son Charles later wrote that his father was "threatened with bodily injury, aye, even to the taking of his life."

On Feb. 27, the commission sent its rulings to Congress. There was no problem in the Republican-controlled Senate, but late on March 1, House Speaker

Samuel Randall (D-Pa.) banged his gavel to head off demands by some angry fellow Democrats to start a filibuster to delay the results. Rep. George Beebe (D-N.Y.) "came climbing over the tops of desks, knocking books and ink bottles on the floor, [and] shook his fist at the speaker," the Chicago Inter-Ocean wrote.

At 4.05 a.m. on March 2, senators came to the House floor for a joint session of Congress. Five minutes later, the president of the Senate announced Hayes had won the presidency, 185 electoral votes to 184. Hayes received word of his victory by telegram while on a train to Washington. The next day — a day before the official start of his presidency, which fell on a Sunday— he took his first oath of office in the Red Room in the Grant White House.

What wasn't reported was that allies of Hayes had begun secret meetings with some Southern Democrats. On April 24, President Hayes announced the withdrawal of federal troops from two Southern statehouses as part of what some historians called the Compromise of 1877. It effectively ended federal Reconstruction, which had already been weakened. as Democrats took control of eight of the 11 former Confederate states.

Black citizens in the South still pressed to save their rights. Bradley would once again stand in their way. In 1883, he wrote the majority Supreme Court opinion striking down the Civil Rights Act of 1875, opening the door for Jim Crow laws and racial segregation in the South. (In 2021, Bradley's alma mater, Rutgers University, removed his name from a campus building.)

To avoid another electoral commission fiasco, Congress passed the Electoral Count Act of 1887, requiring the counting of electoral votes in a ceremony presided over by the vice president.

Bradley's influence rose again on Jan. 6, 2021, when defeated president Donald Trump demanded, without legal basis, that Vice President Mike Pence refuse to accept some states' electoral votes in the ceremony at the Capitol. In a letter to Congress, Pence promised to honor his constitutional duty, noting: "As Supreme Court Justice Joseph Bradley wrote following the contentious election of 1876, the powers of the President of the Senate are merely ministerial ... He is not invested with any authority for making any investigation outside of the Joint Meeting of the two Houses." With Trump-backing insurrectionists attacking the Capitol and shouting, "Hang Mike Pence," the vice president accepted the electoral votes that made Joe Biden president.

In a sense, Joe Bradley was once again our president maker.

# CHAPTER 4

# BANNING BOOKS. AND WALT WHITMAN

By Ronald G. Shafer
*This article was first published in The Washington Post on April 30, 2022*

Long before the current wave of book banning targeted titles including "The 1619 Project" and "Everywhere Babies," Walt Whitman's "Leaves of Grass" was banned from libraries across the United States. The backlash against the poetry book even cost Whitman his federal government job.

Whitman was working as a clerk at the Interior Department in Washington when his boss found a copy of "Leaves of Grass" in his desk and was so outraged by sexually suggestive passages in the book that he fired the poet. "I will not have the author of this book in this department," Interior Secretary James Harlan declared when he dismissed Whitman in 1865.

Whitman's poems about the joys of life contain references to sexual relationships, including same-sex relationships, that were considered shocking at the time. The book stirred protests similar to current outcries over books seen as controversial by some conservative politicians and parents. Challenges to library, school and university books nationwide increased nearly fourfold last year, the American Library Association recently reported. Many banned books deal with gender issues and are "considered to be sexually explicit," the ALA said.

In the mid-1800s, public libraries refused to buy Whitman's "Leaves of Grass" for similar reasons. At the Harvard College library, the only copy was removed from the shelves "and kept under lock and key with other tabooed books," Justin Kaplan wrote in "Walt Whitman. A Life." Yale University's president compared Whitman's poems to "walking naked through the streets."

Whitman self-published the first edition of "Leaves of Grass" in 1855 in his hometown of Brooklyn, N.Y. (it would join New York City in 1898), printing about 800 copies. Its 12 poems were written in free verse, meaning they didn't rhyme. The poet viewed himself as the voice of the American working man. The first poem begins:

*I celebrate myself,*
*And what I assume you shall assume,*
*For every atom belonging to me as good belongs to you*

One reviewer labeled the book "a mass of filth." Ralph Waldo Emerson — the leading poet of the day — disagreed, writing to the 36-year-old Whitman about the book: "I find it the most extraordinary piece of wit and wisdom America has yet contributed. I greet you at the beginning of a great career."

But even Emerson had qualms about an expanded edition in 1856 and a commercially published version in 1860 with 178 poems. Whitman added such sensual poems as "Children of Adam ("*The female form approaching, I pensive, love-flesh tremulous aching*") and "Calumus," which spoke of a youth "*silently approaching and seating himself near, that he may hold me by my hand.*" (Whitman is believed to have been gay.)

In a decidedly mixed review, the New York Times wrote of Whitman's 1860 version, "If possible, he is more reckless and vulgar than in his two former publications. ... Yet it would be unjust to deny the evidence of remarkable power which are presented in this work." The 1860 edition also included the patriotic poem "I Hear America Singing."

In late 1862, as the Civil War raged, Whitman went to the front to help care for his brother, a Union officer who had been wounded in the Battle of Fredericksburg in Virginia. The Cleveland Daily Leader reported the next year that Whitman "is now living in Washington City and having left off writing bad poetry he makes gruel for the sick and wounded soldiers in the hospitals."

FIGURE 5: WALT WHITMAN

In January 1865, Whitman landed a job as a "second class" clerk at the Interior Department's Bureau of Indian Affairs office in the big Patent Office Building. His pay was $1,200 a year, equal to about $22,000 now. "It is easy enough — I take things very easy — the rule is to come at 9 and go at 4 — but I don't come at 9, and only stay till 4 when I want," Whitman wrote to his mother, adding, "I have been sent for by the cashier to receive my PAY for the arduous & invaluable service I have already rendered to the government."

He became an admirer of President Abraham Lincoln. "I see the president almost every day" in the city, he wrote. "What I really like about Lincoln is that there is such a lot of him — Not mere flabby flesh and squashy pulp, but regular downright grit."

When Whitman learned that Lincoln had been assassinated on April 14, 1865, he was at his mother's house in Brooklyn, where he noticed lilacs blooming outside the door. In homage to the fallen president, he wrote the poems "When Lilacs Last in the Dooryard Bloom'd" and "O Captain! My Captain!"

In May 1865, Harlan, a former Republican U.S. senator from Iowa and a devout Methodist, took over as interior secretary. An employee informed Harlan that one of his clerks was the author of an "immoral book." One night, "Harlan was walking around the empty desks at the Patent Office when he found a marked-up copy of the 1860 version of 'Leaves of Grass' in Whitman's desk," Garrett Peck wrote in his book "Walt Whitman in Washington, D.C."

On June 30, Whitman received a one-line memo from Harlan: "The Services of Walter Whitman of New York as a Clerk in the Indian Office will be dispensed with from and after this date." Whitman was fired under a new order by Harlan to oust those who "do not come within the rules of decorum & propriety prescribed by a Christian civilization." Friends appealed on the poet's behalf, but Harlan declared, "If the President of the United States should order his reinstatement, I would resign sooner than I would put him back."

"Our eccentric fellow citizen Walt Whitman has lost his position in the Interior Department at Washington under the general order discharging immoral persons," the Brooklyn Eagle reported. The paper added that Whitman quickly got a clerk job in the attorney general's office, "where we suppose they are not so particular about morals."

A friend came to the defense of Whitman, who was known for his gray beard and wide-brim hat, in a pamphlet called "The Good Gray Poet." The Washington Star wrote that the pamphlet backing the "smutty poet" aimed to show that "most of the ancient poets were even smuttier than Whitman" and that under Harlan's dictums, Homer, Dante and other historical eminences "would not have been eligible to office in the Interior Department."

At the attorney general's office, Whitman interviewed Confederate soldiers seeking pardons under President Andrew Johnson's amnesty policies. He published new versions of "Leaves of Grass" in 1867 and 1871. Whitman worked in the new Justice Department and the Treasury Department before suffering a paralytic stroke and moving to Camden, N.J., in 1873.

In 1881, a Boston publisher printed the sixth version of "Leaves of Grass." About the same time, the noted Irish writer Oscar Wilde visited Boston and told the Boston Globe, "Of all our authors, I consider Walt Whitman far the greatest and noblest. Many of his lines are like a blast fresh from Olympus."

The next blast wasn't from Olympus but from Boston District Attorney Oliver Stevens, who in 1882 banned sales of the new edition printed by the Boston publisher, calling it "obscene literature," unless Whitman removed certain material, including the poem "To a Prostitute." Whitman refused and turned to another publisher to circumvent the ban. The first printing, advertised as "The Suppressed Book," sold out on the first day.

Whitman died in March 1892 at age 72. "Leaves of Grass" remained controversial for decades. It was again in the news in 1998 when it was reported that President Bill Clinton had given a copy of the book to the White House intern Monica Lewinsky.

Today, "Leaves of Grass" is considered one of the greatest books ever written. In the end, the eccentric Washington bureaucrat who wrote a book banned in Boston and in libraries nationwide is widely known as "America's Poet."

# SECTION 2

# NEW NEWS IS OLD NEWS

# CHAPTER 5

# A FORMER PRESIDENT STANDS TRIAL

By Ronald G. Shafer
*This article was first published in The Washington Post on 11/06/2023*

The combative former president's trial is shaping up to be "a legal battle that will make political history." That was the judgment of the New York Times in a headline when Theodore Roosevelt went on trial in a Syracuse, N.Y., courtroom more than a century ago.

Since then, no former U.S. president has testified as a defendant in a court trial. Until now.

Donald Trump is scheduled to testify soon in a New York courtroom in a state $250 million civil fraud case against him and his company. (He also faces 91 felony charges in other cases against him.)

In 1915, Roosevelt was on trial for libel. Like Trump, who is seeking a return to the White House, Roosevelt was trying to hold onto his political influence after losing a presidential election — in 1912 as a candidate for his Progressive Party, also known as the Bull Moose Party.

Trump, who has denounced the fraud charges as a political "witch hunt," could be as volatile on the stand as Roosevelt was, but whether he will be as effective remains to be seen. The libel charge arose out of a 1914 election in New York, where Roosevelt was once governor. The former president had issued a statement condemning an "alliance of corruption" between the Republican and Democratic party machines.

He singled out William Barnes Jr., the Republican state chairman, as "a political boss of the most obnoxious type." Barnes, the publisher of the Albany Evening Journal, sued Roosevelt for $50,000 in damages, equal to nearly $1.5 million today.

When the trial began on April 19, 1915, there was speculation that Roosevelt might run for president again the next year. "This time he had come to Syracuse to defend his honor and perhaps complete one last seemingly quixotic quest to reclaim his political prestige," Dan Abrams and David Fisher wrote in their 2019 book, "Theodore Roosevelt for the Defense."

Under the law then, Roosevelt had to prove allegations he made against Barnes were true. On the trial's second day, the ex-president took the stand to do just that, relating a conversation he once had with Barnes about how New York's state party machines operated.

"He told me," snapped Roosevelt ("as he bit off every word and shot out his chin like a bulldog," the New York Sun reported). "He told me that the people were not fit to govern themselves; that they must be run by party organizations." From his seat opposite Roosevelt, the Sun wrote, "Mr. Barnes quivered with cold rage and looked as though he could have leaped straight at the man from whose lips words of denunciation and insinuation were pouring in a perfect stream."

Roosevelt sparred from the stand with Barnes's lawyer, William Ivins. "Hold on," Ivins objected during Roosevelt's testimony, the New York World reported. "You are making an address to the jury."

"'No I am not,' fairly shrieked Roosevelt, half rising from his seat and shaking his fist," the paper reported. Ignoring the lawyer, Roosevelt continued on a tirade about Barnes, the World wrote: "He turned to the jury, gesticulated with his hands, then showed his teeth and shot out his words like explosive bullets directly into their ears."

FIGURE 6: THEODORE ROOSEVELT WITH NEWSPAPERMEN IN SYRACUSE

Over the ex-president's eight days of testimony, Ivins pressed Roosevelt on why he had continued to deal with Barnes and other political bosses as governor and even president. Roosevelt, who had been his own star witness in winning a 1913 libel suit he brought against a Michigan newspaper, was ready. "I met and found most had a double character — a Dr. Jekyll and a Mr. Hyde," he said. "Few were wholly evil. My constant effort was to appeal to the side that was decent and get them to act rightly."

Roosevelt's defense team called witnesses who testified that Barnes controlled and profited from certain government printing contracts. On May 4, Assistant Navy Secretary Franklin D. Roosevelt, a former New York state lawmaker, testified that Barnes abused his power to win political favors. "Franklin D. really helped," the Washington Herald reported, with "Theodore sitting alert and smiling as his 'fifth cousin by blood and nephew in law' gave his testimony.

Barnes testified for three hours, denying claims of political abuses and illegal actions. Finally, Ivins addressed the jurors. "This is not a political controversy," Ivins said, nodding toward the former president. "The defendant is within the law just the same as anybody else." But he argued that it was Roosevelt, not Barnes, who had the "Jekyll and Hyde personality." He concluded that there was "not one iota of evidence that showed a corrupt machine ruled government."

Roosevelt's lawyer, John Bowers, told the jury the lawsuit was "a proposed act of the machine to destroy Mr. Roosevelt's usefulness to the people of the nation. ... Stand for him; stand for the people; give no vote to accomplish the purpose sought by this action!" He urged the jury to meet its responsibility, "and then Theodore Roosevelt will remain a power for good during his allotted period of life." Bowers concluded by reading President Abraham Lincoln's Gettysburg Address — out of a book published by the wife of presiding Judge William Andrews.

On May 21, after 39 ballots and an overnight lockdown, the jurors hadn't reached a final verdict, the jury foreman told the court, because one juror was holding out for requiring Roosevelt and Barnes to share trial expenses.

Before dawn on May 22, the New York World reported, the holdout juror — Edward Burns, a trolley motorman — was washing his face when he suddenly wheeled around and told the foreman, "I have been thinking this thing over all night, haven't had a wink of sleep, and I've made up my mind." At 4:50 a.m. the jury took another vote.

That day, the jury reported its verdict. "The Barnes-Roosevelt suit came to an end this morning with a complete victory for Theodore Roosevelt after 42 hours and 15 minutes of deliberation," the World reported.

The scenes "which followed the recording of the verdict are probably without parallel in American court history," the New York Times reported. "More than anything else it resembled the headquarters of a successful candidate on election night."

Before the court was adjourned, Roosevelt "was out of his seat and receiving congratulations," the Times said. "He pushed through the crowd to foreman [Warren] Somers and shook his hand violently. 'Somers,' he shouted, slapping the foreman on the back, 'If you can stand it, I want us all to have our picture taken.'"

The ex-president gathered the jurors in an adjoining room, the Times reported, "and gave a typical Rooseveltian reception, making a speech in a voice that he seemed to be able to control only with difficulty."

The verdict revived calls for Roosevelt to run for president again in 1916 against Woodrow Wilson. But it didn't happen. He dropped out of a nomination vote at the Republican convention and refused his old Bull Moose Party's nomination, declaring, "I am out of politics."

On Jan. 6, 1919, Roosevelt died at age 60. The trial victory was his last hurrah.

# CHAPTER 6

# STORMY SEX SCANDALS

By Ronald G. Shafer
*This article was first published in The Washington Post on Oct. 2, 2018*

The Republican presidential candidate's affair could be exposed before the election, so the other woman's silence was bought. Another woman wrote a tell-all book about her love life with the same married man. Long before Donald Trump and Stormy Daniels, there was President Warren G. Harding, whose sexual dalliances made history.

In 1920, the Republicans nominated Harding, a senator from Ohio, to run against Democratic Gov. James Cox, also of Ohio, and his running mate Franklin Delano Roosevelt. Only then did GOP leaders learn their handsome, white-mane standard-bearer had some kinky skeletons in his closet. One was a long-running affair with Carrie Fulton Phillips, the wife of the head of a department store in Marion, Ohio, where Harding was a newspaper publisher.

FIGURE 7: PRESIDENT WARREN G. HARDING

The affair had cooled, and now Phillips threatened to release some steamy love letters, unless she was paid. In one letter, Harding wrote his lover that he longed to see her so much "I feel that there will never be any relief until I take a long, deep, wild draught on your lips and then bury my face on your pillowing breasts."

That was one of the milder letters.

The illicit affair could sink a presidential candidate. So the Republican Party paid Phillips and her husband $20,000 and sent them on an all-expenses paid voyage overseas until the election was over.

Today that $20,000 would be worth about $250,000. That is nearly double the $130,000 Trump paid Daniels before the 2016 presidential election to keep quiet about their alleged affair. And she did not get a free trip.

On Tuesday, Daniels published her memoir "Full Disclosure," which includes details of her Trump tryst. It follows the lead of Nan Britton, with whom Harding was having an affair when he was elected president with a campaign promise "to return America to normalcy."

Britton, who was three decades younger than the 54-year-old Harding, also was the mother of their child, a daughter whom the president never saw. The couple had sex throughout the White House, frequently in a very large cupboard near the president's office. While this was going on, the Secret Service kept close watch for Harding's ever-suspicious wife, Florence, who was known as "the Duchess."

The genial Harding was a popular president. He boasted about what would prove to be a short-lived economic recovery. He supported tax cuts for businesses and the rich, backed higher tariffs and supported limits on immigration. The president largely ignored the details of government. When his Interior Secretary Albert Fall brought him an executive order to secretly transfer some U.S. Navy oil reserves in Wyoming to the Interior Department, Harding signed the order without bothering to read most of it.

The federal oil lands were in a place called Teapot Dome. Fall was taking bribes to allow private oil companies to drill on the property. In 1922, Harding suddenly found his administration under an initial investigation by Congress into the brewing Teapot Dome scandal.

To get away from Washington, in the summer of 1923 Harding and his wife took a goodwill trip to the territory of Alaska and then went by train down to California. Harding fell ill and in San Francisco, on Aug. 2, 1923, the president died of a sudden heart attack.

He was 57 years old. An FBI agent accused Florence Harding of poisoning her husband out of jealousy over his affairs, but never produced any evidence.

Most of the scandals of sex and corruption in Harding's administration did not become fully known until after his death. Fall was convicted of bribery in 1929. Two years earlier, Britton published a best-selling book about her affair with the late president and their child. Britton was angered because she was not included in Harding's will and payments for their child were stopped. Harding supporters called Britton's kiss-and-tell book fiction and fake news.

It was not until 2015 that modern DNA testing proved Britton's claim that Harding was the father of their child. In 2014 the hot love letters of Harding and Britton were published over the objections of Harding's descendants.

In the end, Harding left a legacy that was a cautionary warning for future philanderers in chief: Hell hath no fury like another woman scorned.

(In June 2024, Trump was convicted in New York on felony charges of falsifying business records to hide his payment to Daniels.)

# CHAPTER 7

# THE PRESIDENT'S PAPERS ARE MISSING

By Ronald G. Shafer
*This column was first published in The Washington Post on August 27, 2022*

When President George Washington left office in 1797, he took his presidential papers with him. Federal agents never searched his Mount Vernon home in Virginia. The papers belonged to the former president and not to the government.

As former president Donald Trump has discovered, a lot has changed since then. Today, presidential papers are considered public property and are overseen by the National Archives after a president leaves office. This month the FBI seized boxes of documents, including some top-secret papers, at Trump's Mar-a-Lago estate in Florida — a search justified by the FBI in court filings  by 184 classified documents he failed to turn over when he first left the White House. Trump reportedly has told friends he considers the documents "mine."

Until the 1970s, former presidents could do pretty much whatever they wanted with their presidential papers. That often was a problem. Some papers "were purposely destroyed, while others fell victim to chance destruction," concluded a 1978 congressional study. "Others have been scattered to the four winds."

As the nation's first president, Washington set the precedent. He planned to construct a building at Mount Vernon to store his papers, but he didn't get it done. On the last day of his life in late 1799, according to Mount Vernon's historians, Washington told his secretary Tobias Lear, "I find I am going, my breath cannot continue long … arrange & record all my late Military letters & papers — arrange my accounts & settle my books."

Washington bequeathed his papers to a nephew, Supreme Court Justice Bushrod Washington. The justice loaned many of the documents to Chief Justice

John Marshall, who was writing a biography of the first president. The nephew later lamented in a letter to James Madison that Marshall had stored some papers where they were "extensively mutilated by rats and otherwise injured by damp."

Meanwhile, after her husband died, Martha Washington burned most of the letters  the two had exchanged. "Only a few are known to remain, including two, both tender and fraught, that George Washington wrote just before he left for war," The Washington Post reported in 2015.

John Adams, the second president, and his son President John Quincy Adams both kept detailed records, which heirs later donated to the state of Massachusetts. But after that, the fate of presidential papers was unpredictable.

When President John Tyler of Virginia left office in 1845, most of his papers were moved to a bank in Richmond. After the Civil War began, Tyler died in 1862 on his way to join the Confederate Congress. His papers in Richmond were destroyed in April 1865 when rebel forces set the city on fire to keep it out of Union hands. The rest of Tyler's papers "were left in the Tyler home, Sherwood Forest, which was occupied and ransacked by both Union and Confederate forces several times," the congressional study said.

Most of the late President Zachary Taylor's papers were destroyed when Union troops occupied his son's Louisiana home in 1862. After Abraham Lincoln was assassinated in 1865, his son Robert Todd Lincoln "destroyed many of his father's papers — those he considered useless — before placing the remainder in the Library of Congress," the report said. The Lincoln papers weren't made public until 1947.

President Ulysses S. Grant had a hard time keeping track of his papers. "The only place I ever found in my life to put a paper so as to find it again was either a side coat-pocket or the hands of a clerk more careful than myself," he wrote. As a result, Grant simply lost many of his presidential papers.

President Chester A. Arthur hated the idea of journalists prying into his affairs. The day before his death in November of 1886, "he instructed his son to destroy" his presidential papers, the congressional researchers wrote. "Three large garbage cans were used to burn up the bulk of the Presidential papers."

President Grover Cleveland didn't care much about preserving papers in his two nonconsecutive terms. He regarded any papers addressed to him as his private property, he said, "and if I saw fit to destroy them, no one could complain." Cleveland lost track of many of his papers after leaving office in 1897 and gave away some other documents to autograph seekers.

After President Warren G. Harding died of a heart attack in 1923, his wife, Florence, "destroyed many papers that might have been embarrassing to Harding's memory," the congressional report said.

It didn't help. Nan Britton, Harding's former secretary, claimed in a tell-all book he fathered her child. DNA confirmed his paternity in 2015.

President Calvin Coolidge kept diligent records, which were overseen by one of his assistants, Edward T. Clark. Later, Clark wrote that Coolidge wanted every paper in his so-called personal files destroyed.

"There would have been nothing preserved if I had not taken some things out on my own responsibility," Clark said.

Some presidents went to great efforts to preserve their papers. In the early 1900s, Theodore Roosevelt and William Howard Taft arranged presidential collections that were passed on to heirs and then provided to the Library of Congress. The Taft papers totaled more than 700,000 documents.

Finally, President Franklin D. Roosevelt set the precedent of donating his records to the National Archives and Records Administration. He also established a presidential library. Roosevelt modeled his library after the first presidential library, the Rutherford B. Hayes Presidential Library & Museums, which opened in Fremont, Ohio, in 1916 with papers held in trust after Hayes left office in 1881.

FDR opened his library in Hyde Park, N.Y., on June 30, 1941. "As President, I accept this newest house in which the people's record is preserved," he said. The first day 161 people paid 25 cents each (about $5 now) to visit the library, the Associated Press reported.

The government began designating secret documents as classified just before World War II. All presidents from FDR turned over their papers to the government until Richard M. Nixon tried to keep control of some Watergate material after he resigned in 1974.

Nixon eventually relinquished 42 million pages of documents after Congress passed legislation culminating with the Presidential Records Act of 1978 making the papers of presidents and vice presidents government property.

Trump is the first former chief executive since Nixon to try to keep personal possession of presidential documents.

During House debate on the 1978 law, first-term Rep. Dan Quayle (R-Ind.) suggested the preservation requirements also "should apply to congressmen." Rep. Allen Ertel (D-Pa.) replied, "I might say, Mr. Quayle, there is one thing you have to remember. … I cannot imagine a historian being interested in the papers of a freshman Congressman."

Quayle, of course, later became vice president under President George H.W. Bush.

# CHAPTER 8

# THE OLDEST PRESIDENTIAL CANDIDATE

By Ronald G. Shafer
*This article was first published in The Washington Post on November 12, 2023*

He was the oldest man who had ever run for president, and the demands for him to step aside due to his advanced age grew louder and more forceful. The man was William Henry "Old Tippecanoe" Harrison, the Whig Party candidate in 1840. He was 67.

"Give him a barrel of hard cider and settle a pension of two thousand a year on him," one Baltimore newspaper columnist wrote, "and take my word for it, he will sit the remainder of his days in his log cabin." Instead, the Whigs mounted the first modern presidential campaign, with nationwide rallies and speeches, that used the attacks to catapult "Granny" Harrison into the White House.

If President Biden is reelected, he'd start his next term at 82. Polls show widespread concern about Biden's age and his likely rematch with 77-year-old Republican Donald Trump, who was the second-oldest president at the start of his term. But the Democratic Party establishment continues to support Biden, just as the Whigs did with Harrison in 1840.

The attacks on Old Tippecanoe began soon after the Whigs nominated the former general, a hero in the War of 1812, at its convention in Harrisburg, Pa., to run against 58-year-old President Martin Van Buren. Previously, the oldest president to take office was 61-year-old Andrew Jackson. Democrats quickly labeled the Whigs "Grannycrats."

In early 1840, Thomas Elder, a Whig Party leader, had an idea. Instead of fighting the old-man image, he decided to portray Harrison as the poor man's champion, living as a simple farmer in a log cabin and drinking hard cider, the people's drink. No matter that the old general grew up on the prestigious Berkeley Planation in

Virginia, the son of a wealthy signer of the Declaration of Independence, and now lived in a mansion in North Bend, Ohio. Or that he didn't drink hard cider.

Until then, political parties didn't conduct national rallies, and it was deemed improper for presidential candidate to deliver campaign speeches. Nevertheless, the Whigs mounted "log cabin and hard cider" rallies across the country. On Feb. 22, George Washington's birthday, thousands of people poured into Columbus, Ohio, for a parade featuring log cabins on wheels, marching bands and free cider. The colorful parade spurred one spectator, Alexander Coffman Ross, to write a song about Harrison and his running mate, former senator John Tyler of Virginia.

"What has caused the great commotion, motion, motion, our country through?" the song went. "It is the ball a-rolling on for Tippecanoe and Tyler too." Tippecanoe and Tyler Too became the campaign's theme and remains one of the most famous campaign slogans.

Log cabin fever spread across the nation. "The prairies are on fire," a Cleveland newspaper wrote. More than 60,000 people jammed into Boston for a five-mile parade. A parade in Baltimore by the Whig Young Men featured a rolling log cabin with a live eagle perched on top. In Springfield, Ill., state lawmaker Abraham Lincoln spoke for Harrison from the back of a horse-drawn wagon. Women became involved in a presidential campaign for the first time, waving white handkerchiefs. There was a Log Cabin newspaper edited by Horace Greeley, the future founder of the New York Tribune.

Meanwhile, Whigs sought to create a national image of Harrison as a young army hero. One poster featured a portrait of Harrison at age 27 — one that had been doctored years later by the artist Rembrandt Peale, who painted a military uniform over Harrison's original civilian clothes. A lithograph by Nathaniel Currier showed Harrison as a dashing figure in a black suit and cape against a purple sky.

FIGURE 8: WILLIAM HENRY HARRISON

Harrison didn't take part in any of these celebrations. He stayed home and answered letters from voters. Then a voter in Oswego, N.Y., complained he had written Harrison but received a response from a Whig committee. The Democratic press jumped on the case.

"HORRID BARBARITY" screamed a headline in the Washington Globe, the official paper for Van Buren. "We are credibly informed — though we can scarcely believe it, the fact appears so monstrous and is incredible — that the keepers of Gen. Harrison's conscience have carried their barbarous caution so far as to shut up the old gentleman in an Iron Cage." (The Globe's editor, Francis P. Blair, lived across from the White House. Today the Blair House hosts visiting international guests.)

Democratic papers derided Harrison as "General Mum." It was more than he could stand. So he agreed to speak at a remembrance of the 1813 British siege of his base at Fort Meigs in northern Ohio. On his horse-carriage trip, the old general stayed overnight in Columbus. On the morning of June 6, 1840, on the steps of the National Hotel, Harrison spontaneously gave the first presidential campaign speech in history. "The story goes that I have not only a committee of conscience-keepers but that they put me in a cage," he joked.

On June 11, Harrison gave the first formal presidential campaign speech to 40,000 people at Fort Meigs. To the nation's shock, he also spoke in Cleveland and other Ohio cities. "When was there ever before such a spectacle ... as a candidate for the Presidency, traversing the country, advocating his own claims for that high and responsible station? Never!" exclaimed the Cleveland Advertiser newspaper.

Democrats pointed out that Harrison didn't live in a log cabin and continued to portray him as a feeble old man. To counter the image, Old Tip sometimes rode his white horse right up to the speaker's stand. Other times he rode up in a horse-drawn open carriage and stood to wave to the crowd.

People flocked to see a presidential candidate campaign. Harrison drew 100,000 people in Dayton. "I rise, fellow citizens," he began. A transcriber on the scene reported, "The multitude was here agitated as the sea when the wild wind blows upon it, and it was a full five minutes before the tumult of joy at seeing and hearing the next President of the United States could be calmed."

Van Buren declined to join Harrison on the stump, considering it beneath the dignity of a president. The nation was in an economic decline, and Harrison won the electoral college 234 to 60. Democrats were shocked. "That the American people should have preferred an incapacitated old man ... is indeed a phenomenon that occasions no little regret," the Richmond Enquirer wrote.

In early 1841, Harrison spoke in Cincinnati as he boarded a boat for the first leg of his trip to Washington. "Fellow citizens, perhaps this may be the last time I may have the pleasure of speaking to you on Earth or seeing you," he said.

On Feb. 9, his 68th birthday, Old Tippecanoe became the first president-elect to arrive in Washington by train. On a cold and windy March 4, a coatless Harrison gave the longest inauguration speech in history, one hour and 45 minutes. Exactly one month later, the oldest president became the first commander in chief to die in office. (He remained the oldest president until Ronald Reagan.) The official cause was pneumonia — brought on by his underdressed inauguration, the legend goes, or possibly by a subsequent rainstorm — but a 2014 University of Maryland research report concluded he likely drank contaminated water from the White House tap.

Vice President Tyler became America's 10th president. At 51, he was the youngest U.S. president to date.

# CHAPTER 9

# THE LONGEST VOTE FOR HOUSE SPEAKER

By Ronald G. Shafer
*This article was first published in The Washington Post on December 30, 2022*

For the first time in exactly 100 years, the U.S. House of Representatives may need more than one round of voting to elect a speaker when the new Congress convenes on Tuesday.

But a few extra rounds of balloting would be a far cry from the nearly two months and 133 votes the House took to choose its leader in 1856 — the longest and most contentious speaker election in its history.

The race pitted antislavery Rep. Nathaniel "Bobbin Boy" Banks, a member of the nativist American Party from Massachusetts, against candidates who were open to expanding slavery to new states and territories. The debate raged on amid mounting violence between proslavery and antislavery settlers in "Bleeding Kansas."

Today, Minority Leader Kevin McCarthy (R-Calif.) is struggling to win enough votes to be elected speaker when Republicans take narrow control of the House, as he faces opposition from some right-wing members of his party. As a result, it may take more than one ballot for anyone to gain the 218 votes, or the majority of votes cast for candidates, needed to win the speakership. McCarthy has warned fellow Republicans against a floor fight, saying, "If we play games on the floor, Democrats could end up picking who the speaker is."

The last time a speaker election took more than one ballot was in 1923, when Speaker Frederick Gillett (R-Mass.) was reelected on the ninth ballot.

But the longest speaker vote began on Dec. 3, 1855, when the 34th Congress convened. Democrats controlled the Senate, but no party controlled the House after the disintegration of the Whig Party. About a third of House members were Democrats. The rest belonged to a mix of parties, including the new Republican

Party. Many were members of the secretive American Party, also known as the Know Nothing party.

On the first day, 21 candidates vied for the speakership. Four votes were taken. The early leader was Rep. William Richardson (D-Ill.), who favored permitting future states to allow slavery, with 74 votes, far short of the 113 needed for a majority. A few days later, antislavery members lined up behind the American Party's "Bobbin Boy" Banks, who as a boy worked in a textile factory carrying bobbins of thread to the women who operated the looms. The 39-year-old Banks, the New York Herald reported, was "a good looking man" with a stiff, puritanical manner who "is even said never to have drank a glass of liquor in his life."

On the 33rd tally, in mid-December, Banks received 100 votes to Richardson's 73, and the deadlock continued into the new year as the slavery debate heated up. "This is not a mere contest as to a Speaker of the House; it is but an incident in a long and arduous struggle which is to determine whether slavery will be the pole star of our National career," Horace Greeley's New York Tribune wrote.

The fiery floor debate turned violent outside the Capitol in late January as Greeley, who supported Banks, was leaving a House session. A burly man approached the Tribune publisher and "struck me a stunning blow on the right side of my head and followed it by two or three more, as rapidly as possible," Greeley wrote. The attacker was anti-Banks Rep. Albert Rust (D-Ark.).

FIGURE 9: HOUSE SPEAKER NATHANIEL BANKS

Finally, on Feb. 1, 1856, Democrats adopted a new strategy. First, they backed a new speaker candidate, proslavery Rep. William Aiken Jr. (D-S.C.), the 50-year-old son of railroad magnate William Aiken Sr., after whom Aiken, S.C., was named. Second, Democratic leaders announced that they would propose the next day a previously rejected resolution to elect a speaker with only a plurality vote. Under this plan, if a majority of members failed to elect a speaker in three consecutive votes, the candidate who got the most votes on a fourth tally would win.

Aiken was sure to win over enough Southern House members to gain a plurality and the speakership, newspapers reported. "We think we can count 109 votes for Mr. Aiken, if jealousy or something else does not defeat him," a Washington Star correspondent wrote. That night, Democratic President Franklin Pierce congratulated Aiken in advance on his victory.

On Saturday, Feb. 2, in Washington, "the sun rose on an excited city," the New Orleans Picayune reported. That afternoon, Rep. Samuel Smith (D-Tenn.) proposed the plurality resolution, "intimating his belief it would elect Mr. Aiken." The resolution passed. "The excitement now became very great," the Picayune wrote. On the third vote, Banks led Aiken 103 votes to 95, short of a majority. Some of the remaining speaker candidates then dropped out, with Aiken poised to scoop up their backers.

The fourth vote — with the plurality resolution in place — began. As the clerk tallied the total, "the excited crowd on the floor and in the galleries looked on in silence," the Picayune reported. "The suspense at this crisis was agonizing. Every eye turned and every ear inclined with intense interest towards the clerk's desk to hear the result."

Just before 7 p.m., the clerk announced the total: 103 votes for Banks, 100 for Aiken. Some lawmakers who had been expected to switch to Aiken had not come through. "As the result was announced, the audience in the galleries manifest their joy by peal after peal of deafening cheers," the Picayune wrote. "The ladies waved their handkerchiefs wildly and clapped, and [anti-Banks] gentlemen stamped and raved, and swore."

Banks, with his "thick dark hair swept to one side and a prominent mustache obscuring his upper lip," addressed members from the speaker's chair, according to the House's official history. He noted that his job was "now environed with unusual difficulties."

The difficulties increased. In mid-May, Sen. Charles Sumner (R-Mass.) spoke against allowing slavery in Kansas while chastising a senator from South Carolina who supported "the harlot, Slavery." Three days later, as Sumner worked at his Senate desk, Rep. Preston Brooks (D-S.C.) approached and accused Sumner of speaking "libel" against his state. Brooks began beating Sumner on the head with his metal-tipped cane. Sumner was knocked to the floor, as bystanders shouted, "Hit him, Brooks. He deserves it." Some senators finally restrained Brooks, and others carried Sumner out with his head bleeding. The House, with Banks's support, voted to expel Brooks, who resigned but was soon reelected.

Banks, who never embraced the Know Nothings' anti-immigrant stance, served one term as speaker and was then elected governor of Massachusetts as a Republican.

In the House's 234-year history, 14 speaker votes have required multiple ballots. With the rise of the two-party system, only two have come after 1856.

The job of House speaker is often a frustrating one, but not as frustrating as another top federal post, according to late House Speaker John Nance "Cactus Jack" Garner (D-Tex.), who said: "Worst damn fool mistake I ever made was letting myself be elected vice president of the United States. Gave up the second most important job in government for eight long years as [Franklin] Roosevelt's spare tire."

# CHAPTER 10

# DISORDER IN THE HOUSE

By Ronald G. Shafer

Now members of Congress are throwing elbows and threatening fights. The tantrums are throwbacks to the days when lawmakers knocked heads and even drew weapons.

In the mad-cap Republican-controlled House Rep. Tim Burchett (R-Tenn.) accused Rep. Kevin McCarthy (R-Calif.) of elbowing him with a "clean shot to the kidneys" as they passed each other in a crowded House hallway in November 2023. Did not, McCarthy responded. At a Senate hearing Sen. Markwayne Mullin (R-Okla.) challenged a witness to a fistfight and started offering campaign donors a shirt that says "Anytime, Anyplace."

The bad old days started in 1798 when Connecticut Rep. Roger Griswold thrashed Vermont Rep. Matthew Lyon with a hickory cane for the "gross indecency" of spitting tobacco juice in his face while on the House floor. Lyon defended himself with a pair of fireplace tongs.

FIGURE 10: THE CANING OF CONGRESSMAN LYON

In early 1837, Rep. Henry Wise (W.-Va.), who could spit tobacco at 15 feet, was carrying a gun at a contentious House hearing and assumed a very hostile witness was, too. Wise said later he closely watched the motion of the witness's right elbow and " had it moved one inch, he had died on the spot."

Wise also was fast with his fists. In 1841, he slugged Rep. Edward Stanly (W-NC.), and a House clerk reported "'nearly all the members'" began pummeling each other in a wild melee," Joanne B. Freeman wrote in her 2018 book "The Field of Blood. Violence In Congress."

An 1854 clash on the House floor seemed to provide a model for peaceful compromise. Rep. William Churchwell (D-Tenn.) accused Rep. William Cullom (W-Tenn.) of inserting "infamously false" statements about him in the Congressional Globe, the predecessor to the Congressional Record. In response, Cullom "rose from his seat and rushed towards" Churchwell "with threatening gestures," the Tennessean newspaper reported.

Churchwell then reached for a gun in his pocket, but Rep. Burton Craig (D-NC.) grabbed his hand. The New York Times called the fight an "unfortunate and disgraceful scene," and suggested a vote to see "who among the members are in favor of converting the Representative Chamber into a shooting-gallery, and who are not."

Churchwell and Cullom apologized to the House the next day. To ease tensions, Rep. Preston Brooks (D-SC.) proposed two resolutions: One that "any member who brings into this House a concealed weapon shall be expelled," and another that the Sergeant-at-Arms "shall cause to be erected a suitable rack in the rotunda, where members who are addicted to the carrying of concealed weapons shall be required to place them before entering this hall."

"The reading of the resolutions," according to the Globe, "was greeted with much applause and laughter." Tensions were eased. But the fighting didn't stop.

What the House archives call "the most infamous floor brawl " in House history took place about 2 a.m. on Feb. 6, 1858 during a debate on a pro-slavery clause to the Kansas statehood proposals. A reporter for the Albany Evening Journal chronicled the clash blow by blow.

Rep. Galusha Grow (R-Pa.) was walking back from the Democratic side of the chamber when he objected to a Democratic motion. "Damn you, go over to your own side if you want to object," growled Rep. Laurence Keitt (D-S.C.), who was "unusually ostentatious and noisy," the Journal reported. "I'll teach you," yelled Keitt, who grabbed Grow by the neck. Grow responded with "a heavy blow with his right fist," knocking Keitt lto the floor.

"And now the melee became general. As Keitt fell, Grow was seized by a half dozen Southerners," the Journal reported. "In the twinkly of an eye from forty to fifty Republicans came dashing across the hall to the scene." Leading the way was John "Bowie Knife" Potter (R-Wis.), who leapt into the fight "with the bound of a tiger and commenced hitting right and left."

Potter threw his fists toward Ethelbert Barksdale (D-Miss.), who mistakenly thought they came from Rep. Elihu Washburn (W-Ill.) "who just happened to be hovering in that vicinity," the Journal said. In the middle of the scuffle, Potter grabbed Barksdale by the hair, which "proved not to be bona fide hair." It was a wig, which Potter proceeded to tear off. Then Rep. Cadwallader Washburn(R-Wis.), "seeing the bald Barksdale in conflict with his brother, rushed up to strike two blows "on the top of Barksdale's head where the wool ought to grow."

At this point Speaker James Orr (D-S.C.) was pounding his gavel and shouting for order. The burly Sergeant-at-Arms, raising the metallic House mace, "rushed among the strugglingly, surging, tossing members," the Journal reported. Order was restored.

After the House defeated the provision two days later, Rep. Joshua Gibbings (Free Soil-Ohio) said, "I have sat in this House twenty years, and I never saw the slave power so completely baffled and cowed as during the fifteen hours contest."

In early 1861, just before the start of the Civil War, Congress voted to make Kansas a free state. By this time tension was so high, the Alexandria Gazette reported, that "two-thirds of the members of the House go up to the Capitol every day carrying concealed weapons." It wasn't until 1967 that Congress barred lawmakers from carrying firearms onto the floor of the House and Senate.

But sharp elbows are still allowed.

# CHAPTER 11

# A NAPOLEON ANCESTOR STARTED THE FBI

By Ronald G. Shafer
*This article was first published in The Washington Post on Aug. 16, 2022*

The Federal Bureau of Investigation has a French connection: The agency's fore-runner was created in 1908 by Emperor Napoleon Bonaparte's great-nephew, Charles J. Bonaparte, when he was President Theodore Roosevelt's attorney general.

Bonaparte had a reputation for high integrity, an image generally shared over the years by FBI agents. Since the disclosure of the FBI search of former president Donald Trump's home at his Mar-a-Lago Club in Palm Beach, Fla., many Trump backers and Trump himself have been quick to turn on the FBI agents involved, with Trump suggesting, with no basis, they may have "planted" evidence against him.

Recent reporting has revealed the FBI was searching for highly classified documents, some involving nuclear weapons. In his only public statement on the matter, Attorney General Merrick Garland defended FBI agents and federal prosecutors. "I will not stand by silently when their integrity is unfairly attacked," Garland said. "The men and women of the FBI and the Justice Department are dedicated, patriotic public servants."

Before becoming attorney general, Bonaparte had been navy secretary in early 1906 when he expressed concern about whether he was doing a good enough job. Roosevelt wrote back to his fellow progressive Republican, "You are a trump!" — a term for a dependable or admirable person — and disclosed plans to nominate Bonaparte to be attorney general that year.

FIGURE 11: CHARLES BONAPARTE

Bonaparte created the forerunner to the FBI because the Justice Department didn't have its own investigators when enforcing federal laws. As a wealthy lawyer in Baltimore, he had fought corruption as head of the National Civil Service Reform League. When Roosevelt appointed Bonaparte navy secretary, cartoonists were quick to note the 1805 drubbing of Napoleon's French naval fleet by the British in the Battle of Trafalgar off the coast of Spain. One cartoon showed the "Spirit of Napoleon" reading a telegram from Roosevelt, which stated, "I have made your grandnephew Secretary of the Navy"; Napoleon replied, "I hope he does better with ships than I did."

As attorney general, Bonaparte led Roosevelt's trustbusting drive, breaking up such giants as Standard Oil Company. He personally argued dozens of cases before the Supreme Court. The press gave him the nickname "Charlie the Crook Chaser." But when it came to enforcing federal laws, he complained to Congress that the department had "no permanent detective force under its control." Instead, he had to borrow Secret Service agents from the Treasury Department.

In May 1908, Congress banned the outside use of the Secret Service investigators — a move that just so happened to occur after two lawmakers were jailed as the result of such probes. Bonaparte saw his opening. He created a "Special Agent Force" of 31 investigators, including eight former Secret Service agents. He issued an order that "All matters relating to investigations under the Department" will be referred to the chief examiner, Stanley Finch, to decide "whether any member of the force of special agents under his direction is available for the work to be performed." The order was dated July 26, 1908, now considered the birth date of the FBI.

The standards for special agents resembled today's requirements. According to Finch, the Washington Star later reported, the agents "were to be well educated — preferably graduates of some college and members of the bar; they were not to be unusual in appearance, so that they could pass unnoticed in a crowd." In a 1908 report to Congress, Bonaparte declared the force was "absolutely indispensable" to the proper discharge of the Justice Department's duties.

When Bonaparte left office in March 1909 as William Howard Taft moved into the White House, he recommended that the special agents be made a permanent part of the Justice Department. Taft agreed. His attorney general, George Wickersham, soon named the special force the Bureau of Investigation, or the BOI.

Agents initially focused on white-collar crime, such as land and bankruptcy fraud, antitrust violations and "matters relating to the importation of prostitutes." In 1910, agents' duties expanded to include enforcement of the White Slave Traffic Act, also known as the Mann Act, which outlawed transporting women over state lines for "immoral purposes." Over the next few years, the BOI force grew to more than 300 agents.

In 1919, the agency hired its first African American agent, James Wormley Jones. He was assigned to infiltrate subversive groups. In 1922, Alaska Davidson became the first female special agent. But two years later, the agency's new chief, 29-year-old J. Edgar Hoover, forced her resignation after her boss said he had "no particular work for a woman."

During the 1930s, the agency was called the Division of Investigation (DOI) and gained a reputation for battling organized crime. Legend has it that gangster George Kelly Barnes, known as Machine Gun Kelly, coined the name G-men, or government men, for agents when he shouted, "Don't shoot, G-men!" while being arrested.

In 1935, Congress agreed to Hoover's request to give the unit a new name, the Federal Bureau of Investigation. On March 22, 1935, President Franklin D. Roosevelt signed the bill creating the new name and its motto "Fidelity, Bravery, Integrity."

Hoover served as FBI director until his death in 1972 at age 77. His long tenure was tarnished by racial bigotry and abuses of civil liberties. President Richard M. Nixon, among others, suggested Hoover held onto his post because he had dirt on members of Congress and other powerful people. "He's got files on everybody, damn it," Nixon said.

Today, the FBI has more than 30,000 agents and other professionals. The agency's law enforcement mission ranges from white-collar crime to cybercrime and terrorism — and now to carrying out search warrants at the home of a former president. That's a long way from the 31-man force Charles Bonaparte started 114 years ago.

The former attorney general died at his Bella Vista estate in Maryland in 1921 at age 70. In his obituary, the Baltimore American noted that Bonaparte had a pet peeve about his famous ancestor's reputed short stature, which spawned the Napoleon complex, the theory that some short people try to compensate by being overly aggressive.

"Persons who sought to flatter Mr. Bonaparte by telling him he looked like Napoleon irritated him," the newspaper wrote, "for he knew he was taller."

# CHAPTER 12

# MAKING YOUR TAX PAYMENT PUBLIC

By Ronald G. Shafer
*This article was first published in The Washington Post on April 18, 2022*

As Americans send off their tax returns, they don't have to worry about their neighbors knowing how much they earned or paid. But for a while in the 1920s, everybody's tax payments were public records for all to see. And the richest Americans were not happy about it.

One goal of the 1924 tax publicity law was to show whether wealthy Americans and large corporations were paying their fair share of taxes. Newspapers published big stories on the first release of tax payments. Oil heir John D. Rockefeller Jr. was America's biggest taxpayer, with a tax bill of $7,435,160.41, equal to about $123 million now. Next was automaker Henry Ford, who paid $2,467,400.10, or $41 million today. Douglas Fairbanks and Gloria Swanson were the highest-paying movie stars. Incomes weren't disclosed, though they could be roughly inferred.

The Big Reveal was short-lived. In 1926, Republican President Calvin Coolidge, under pressure from rich taxpayers, got Congress to end the public tax payments.

President Biden, in his fiscal 2023 budget, is proposing a "Billionaire Minimum Income Tax" of 20 percent on households with more than $100 million in both income and "unrealized gains." The proposal wouldn't make tax payments public but seeks to adjust a "tax code that results in America's wealthiest households paying a lower tax rate than working families," the White House said. Critics contend the plan would hurt long-term investments.

Tax payments were secret after the modern federal income tax was established in 1913. But in the early 1920s, reformers began calling for disclosure, as former Republican president Benjamin Harrison had urged in an 1898 speech on the "Obligation of Wealth."

"Each citizen has a personal interest in the tax return of his neighbor," Harrison said. "We are members of a great partnership, and it is the right of each to know what every other member is contributing to the partnership, and what he is taking from it."

In 1924, Coolidge and Treasury Secretary Andrew Mellon, of the ultrawealthy Pittsburgh banking family, got the Republican Congress to cut the top individual tax rate from 58 percent to 46 percent. In return, progressive senators, including some Republicans, won a provision to make all federal tax payments public, arguing that this would deter tax dodgers.

That fall, the Internal Revenue Service's first release of tax payments for 1923 made headlines across the country. Mellon, who had vigorously opposed public release, was reported to have paid $1,178,988 in taxes, equal to $19 million today. Railroad magnate Frederick Vanderbilt paid $800,000 in taxes, equal to $13 million now. Papers also published long lists of payments by local, ordinary taxpayers.

The annual disclosures revealed that, as now, the ultrarich often paid relatively low tax rates after taking legal write-offs. In 1924, Chicago chewing-gum king William Wrigley Jr.'s taxes plummeted to $2,681, or about $44,000 today, from $865,815 in 1923, or $14 million now. Wrigley's representatives said he had "written off certain losses of the last 10 years," the Chicago Tribune reported.

Humorist Will Rogers wrote that for taxpayers, "this publication of amounts" was "a test of their honesty." He concluded that "the income tax has made more liars out of the American people than golf has." To prevent the rich from benefiting from tax loopholes, Rogers suggested, "you should get out a new kind of tax every year or two, so they don't know how to beat it."

FIGURE 12: WILL ROGERS. "THE INCOME TAX HAS MADE MORE LIARS OUT OF THE AMERICAN PEOPLE THAN GOLF HAS."

Not all newspapers joined in the tax dump. The Boston Herald called the exposure "an outrage" that violated taxpayers' privacy. The Minnesota Tribune, in an article headlined "No Aid For Snoopers," vowed to protect the privacy of the ordinary taxpayer: "He ought to be allowed to hug his own little income to his bosom, in glee or sorrow, without the public sniffing around him."

Many papers feared publishing the lists would be illegal. That issue was cleared up in May 1925, when the Supreme Court unanimously ruled that newspapers couldn't be sued for printing the tax lists.

That fall, The Washington Post plunged in, under the headline "Spotlight glares on tax payments for 1924 incomes." Tops in Washington was the paper's own publisher, E.B. McLean, who paid $281,125 in taxes, or $4.6 million now. Coolidge paid $14,091, or $219,000 now. "In several instances men reputed to be wealthy made small returns," the paper reported.

The Post noted that a "striking increase was shown in the number of women making individual returns, evidence of their growth in the business and professional world." Leading the way in Washington was Kate Willard Boyd, from the Willard Hotel family, whose tax payment totaled $31,842, or $528,000 now. The Post also listed in alphabetical order the payments of many city residents, starting with Aussell L. Alden of 809 L St. NW, who paid $58.41 in taxes, equal to $960 today.

The Chicago Tribune's state-by-state stories on the top corporate tax-payers read like a roll call of consumer products such as washing machines and automobiles: "Maytag Highest Iowa Taxpayer," Studebaker "noted in Indiana List," and "Nash Tax Is Largest in Wisconsin."

The Tribune noted that one group of local citizens was missing from taxpayers lists: "The search for incomes of the city's underworld gentry, the beer runners, the bootleggers, crooked politicians, gunmen, gang leaders and their like indicated that, unless they have cheated Uncle Sam, they have no incomes."

The Pittsburgh Courier, a Black newspaper, lamented the lack of African Americans among the high taxpayers. "The most astounding fact" about New York's listing of Black "Harlem millionaires is that there aren't any," the paper said. Later, the Courier reported there was one Black millionaire, Watt Terry, who owned properties in Harlem but lived in Brockton, Mass.

Treasury chief Mellon led the opposition by the wealthy to the disclosures. "There is no excuse for the present publicity provision except the gratification of idle curiosity and the filling of newspaper space," he argued. Many lower-earning taxpayers also protested the public exposure of their payments.

In 1926, at Coolidge's urging, Congress cut the top tax rate again, this time to 25 percent, and repealed the tax disclosures. Sen. George Norris (R-Neb.), a leading proponent of disclosure, predicted the repeal would make it easier "through secret manipulation for big taxpayers to avoid payment of the honest taxes which they owe under the law."

# CHAPTER 13

# ENGLAND'S NEW ROYALTY

By Ronald G. Shafer
*This article was first published in The Washington Post on May 4, 2023*

Nearly 70 years before King Charles III's coronation on May 6 in London's Westminster Abbey, he watched as his mother, Queen Elizabeth II, was crowned in the same hallowed setting. Charles is 74 years old. Elizabeth was 27. And her ceremony was far more ornate than his is expected to be.

On the cold and rainy morning of June 2, 1953, nearly 3 million people lined the streets of London as the dark-haired queen "rode in her golden coach, amid a thunderous tide of cheers" to her coronation, the London Herald Express reported. "All the panoply and colour, the rich warm texture of age-old ceremony formed a brilliant and unforgettable canvas on which were focused the hopes and prayers for the young and beautiful Queen as she took her place in the nation's ancient story of Kingship."

One of the 8,251 people jammed inside the abbey was 78-year-old Prime Minister Sir Winston Churchill. The "proud old lion acclaimed his young Queen today with his eyes brimming with emotion," the Associated Press reported. "The man who served Queen Victoria more than a half century ago repeated once again what for him were magic words, 'God save the Queen.'"

Millions more watched the coronation on the new medium of television. Churchill and other British leaders at first opposed televising the ceremony as undignified. But the British public sided with the queen's husband, Prince Philip, the Duke of Edinburgh, who argued that televising the event would help modernize the monarchy. The British Broadcasting Corp. reported that more than 20 million of Britain's 36 million people watched the telecast, and 11 million listened on radio.

Film of the celebration — which took place five hours ahead of U.S. Eastern time — was flown to ABC-TV, NBC-TV and CBS-TV in New York in time to be shown that same evening. More than 32 million Americans watched the coverage, according to the American Research Bureau. The event was "probably the greatest moment of television's young life," the International News Service reported, spurring sales of TV sets both in the United States and England.

"Don't miss the Coronation. See it Best on RCA VICTOR," blared an ad for a 17-inch black-and-white TV selling for $329.50, equal to about $3,700 now.

President Dwight D. Eisenhower watched part of the coronation on TV at the White House. Eisenhower had met then-Princess Elizabeth when he was supreme commander of Allied forces in Europe during World War II.

At the time of the coronation, the United States was winding up negotiations to end the Korean War. The No. 1 song in both the United States and the United Kingdom was "The Song From Moulin Rouge."

More than 2,000 journalists and 500 photographers from 92 nations covered the coronation. One photographer was a 23-year-old Jacqueline Bouvier, the soon-to-be fiancee of U.S. senator and future president John F. Kennedy. For an article distributed by the Chicago Tribune News Service, Bouvier asked people outside Buckingham Palace: "Do you think Elizabeth will be England's last queen?" The article quoted Alma Santos, a housewife from Cardiff, Wales, who said, "O, I couldn't say. I hope we will have Prince Charles after her, but in future times you never know what will happen, do you?"

Elizabeth was awakened at 6 a.m. on her coronation day, to be given the news of another historic event 4,000 miles away. On May 29, as part of a British expedition, New Zealand beekeeper Edmund Hillary and Nepali-Indian mountaineer Tenzing Norgay had become the first climbers confirmed to reach the summit of 29,000-foot Mount Everest, between Nepal and Tibet. Elizabeth sent congratulations "and retired again," United Press reported.

The top coronation question was what the queen would wear. "The biggest fashion secret of the Coronation was revealed today," the New York Daily News reported. "Queen Elizabeth will wear a white satin dress, glitterly jeweled and embroidered, when she is crowned tomorrow." The dress was embroidered with emblems of Great Britain and the British Commonwealth.

Though Charles has said he plans a less lavish coronation than his mother's, he will lead a three-day celebration fit for a king, including a concert with Katy Perry and Lionel Richie. In 1953, England went all out because Elizabeth's coronation was the first for a queen since Queen Victoria was crowned in 1838. At the time of her coronation, Elizabeth had actually been queen for 16 months since her father, King George VI, died on Feb. 6, 1952.

FIGURE 13: QUEEN ELIZABETH II

The queen, escorted by thousands of military troops marching or on horse-back, paraded to Westminster Abbey in her covered Gold State coach pulled by eight gray horses with such names as Snow White, Tipperary and Eisenhower. Philip wore a blue Navy admiral uniform laden with ribbons and medals. "To a fanfare of trumpets," the AP reported, the queen entered the abbey wearing "a scarlet robe, its long train carried by six maids of honor in white." The ceremony began at 11:15 a.m. with the Archbishop of Canterbury presiding.

Elizabeth initially sat in the Chair of Estate for the "recognition," with the archbishop proclaiming her "our undoubted queen." Then she moved to the King Edward's Chair, made in 1300 for King Edward I, for her anointment with holy oils. Next, she was presented with symbolic items, including a sword with a jeweled scabbard and the "bracelets of sincerity." After donning the Robe Royal of gold cloth, she was given a gold orb and two royal scepters.

Then, "the moment the world awaited came when the Archbishop of Canterbury held high above the Queen's head St. Edward's Crown with its dazzle of diamonds, its arches aglow with pearls and its bejeweled cross," the Derby Evening Telegraph reported. The gold crown, which weighs nearly five pounds, was made in 1661 for King Charles II and is a replica of the crown of the 11th-century king Edward the Confessor.

The archbishop, holding the heavy crown with two hands, gently placed it on Elizabeth's head. She was officially crowned the queen of England. "Out from the abbey flashed a signal, and the guns at the Tower of London, Hyde Park and at Windsor Castle and on the Thames fired royal salutes," the AP reported.

For the first time, she sat on the gold throne to receive homage from her husband and other royals. The abbey rang with shouts of "Long Live Queen Elizabeth."

"With the splendour and solemnity of an historic ritual … Elizabeth II was yesterday crowned queen," the London Daily Telegraph reported. Some American journalists were less reverent. "The British did everything during the Coronation of Queen Elizabeth except sail a battleship into Trafalgar Square at high noon," AP columnist Hal Boyle wrote. The New York Daily News ran a front-page headline declaring: "Long Live Liz."

Finally, after switching to the lighter Imperial Crown, based on the crown made for Queen Victoria's coronation, Elizabeth walked slowly out of the abbey, "her face showing no sign of strain" from the nearly three-hour ceremony "which she had borne with such dignity," the Birmingham Post reported. Now dressed in a purple velvet robe, she returned to her coach for a meandering 4.5-mile, two-hour procession through London streets to Buckingham Palace as spectators cheered.

At the palace, at 5:42 p.m., "her Majesty" came to the balcony and waved to the crowd as 168 Royal Air Force fighter jets flew low overhead in a royal salute. The queen came to the balcony five more times, the last at midnight. "People danced in Piccadilly Circus until 3:30 a.m.," the London Telegraph wrote.

Newspapers reported nearly every movement of 4-year-old Charles. The boy sat on a stool in the Royal Gallery to watch the coronation. "Look, it's Mummy," he said. "Prince Charles, in white shirt and knickers and with his hair scrumptiously parted … sometimes seemed baffled by it all," the Birmingham Evening Despatch wrote. But as he left, "he looked as though he had thoroughly enjoyed his stay. All eyes were upon the little figure as he waved to those about him and disappeared."

The St. Edward's Crown was recently removed from display at the Tower of London in preparation for the coronation of King Charles and Queen Consort Camilla. On May 6, just one month short of 70 years after his mother's coronation, the historic crown will be placed on Charles's head. Then, for the first time at a coronation since his grandfather's in 1937, Westminster Abbey will ring with shouts of "God save the king."

# SECTION 3:

# OLD-TIME MOVIES

# CHAPTER 14

# SHOCKING, SHOCKING MOVIE QUOTES

By Ronald G. Shafer
*This article was first published in The Washington Post on March 9, 2023*

For many of us older movie fans who will tune in to the 95th Academy Awards on Sunday, the classic "Casablanca" — the 1944 winner for best picture — is still the most quotable film of all time. But to many younger people, our favorite references from old movies are going, if not gone, with the wind.

That struck me one evening when my wife, Mary, and I sat down for dinner at a local restaurant. Mary was recovering from a cold that sent her voice several octaves lower. "I'm with Lauren Bacall tonight," I quipped to our waiter.

His blank look spoke volumes. Of all the gin joints, in all the towns, in all the world, I walked into one where the young server had no clue about my reference to the husky-voiced actress of the 1950s. If he got any of my cultural references that night, I would be "shocked, shocked."

FIGURE 14: HUMPHREY BOGART AND INGRID BERGMAN

For the older among us, more and more of our favorite movie catchphrases are ready to board that boat that crosses the historical reference Rubicon, from the realm of witty repartee to cultural oblivion. It's time to "Round up the usual suspects." And when we do, "We're gonna need a bigger boat."

Take the celebrated 1972 movie "The Godfather." You may have noticed that nobody below a certain age winces when you make him "an offer he can't refuse." All I can say is, "Why didn't you come to me first?" I would have told you that, today, even a great "Godfather" reference "sleeps with the fishes."

And it looks like you picked the wrong day to slip in quips from another movie classic "Airplane." Surely, you ask, you can't mean that? Yes, I do. And don't call me Shirley.

When dining with their wives, husbands will have to retire their go-to remark, "I'll have what she's having." Chances are good that the young server has never seen "When Harry Met Sally." There's no point in telling somebody to "Go ahead. Make my day, " when they've never heard of Clint Eastwood as Dirty Harry in "Sudden Impact."

Generational linguistic transitions are nothing new. We all puzzled over the things our parents said when we were "knee-high to a grasshopper."

Now we're the ones struggling to understand some of the phrases and references young people use. They also drop phrases from what they consider to be older movies. "Just keep swimming," "they urge, from "Finding Nemo." And "May the odds ever be in your favor" from "The Hunger Games." And "Chewie, we're home," from "Star Wars: The Force Awakens."

Fortunately, some theatrical references stand the test of time. "All the world's [still] a stage" in the words of William "To be or not to be" Shakespeare. "All that glitters [still] is not gold." And if your joke-telling uncle goes on too long, he'll know what you mean when you say, "Brevity is the soul of wit." But who knows how long Shakespeare will be the king of quotes? As Will himself wrote, "Uneasy lies the head that wears a crown."

So is nothing sacred? "O ye of little faith." The Bible is still a veritable "behemoth" for references, including the word "behemoth," for example. So you can still "eat, drink and be merry." But be warned, "the writing is on the wall."

The time for many of our favorite phrases has come and gone. The cruel fact is these days nobody remembers the Maine and hardly anybody remembers the Alamo. If you can't accept that, then 'You can't handle the truth" "But for those who are determined to declare "I coulda been a contender," I say, "Here's looking at you kid." (Followed by "May the Force be with you."

As for myself, if I stop now, I know I'll regret it. "Maybe not today, and maybe not tomorrow, but soon," and for the rest of my life.

So, "Play it again, Sam" "(Or for purists, just "Play it, Sam.") I will continue to "follow the money" all the way "to infinity and beyond." And if you don't like it, well, "Frankly, my dear, I don't give a damn."

\

# CHAPTER 15

# AN ACADEMY AWARD WINNER GONE WITH THE WIND

By Ronald G. Shafer
*This article was first published in The Washington Post on March 27, 2022*

On the evening of Feb. 29, 1940, actress Hattie McDaniel, with white gardenias in her hair, swept into the Ambassador Hotel's Cocoanut Grove nightclub in Los Angeles for the Academy Awards banquet. That night, she would become the first African American ever to win an Oscar for her role as an enslaved maid in the blockbuster movie "Gone With the Wind."

But the hotel didn't allow the 44-year-old McDaniel to sit at the same table as the film's White cast members. And her historic award for best supporting actress didn't open doors to better movie roles for Black actors, including McDaniel herself. Instead of winning wider success because of her Oscar, she said later, "it was if I had done something wrong."

An African American didn't win a competitive Oscar again until 1964 (James Baskett won an honorary Oscar in 1948 for portraying Uncle Remus), when the best actor award went to Sidney Poitier, who died this year at age 94. It wasn't until 2002 that Halle Berry became the only African American to win the best actress award.

African Americans have won 20 acting Oscars, but as recently as 2015, a call for more diversity began under the banner #OscarsSoWhite. This year, four African Americans are nominated for acting awards, down from nine last year, at Sunday's ceremony at the Dolby Theatre.

McDaniel's rise from poverty to an Academy Award is a story right out of the movies. She grew up in Colorado as the youngest of 13 children. Both her parents had been enslaved; her father was a Baptist minister. She performed in Black minstrel shows before moving to Los Angeles, where she eventually built a movie career in comedies as a sassy maid.

In 1939, a huge opportunity arose. Producer David O. Selznick bought the rights to Margaret Mitchell's best-selling book "Gone With the Wind," about the Old South before and after the Civil War. The heavyset McDaniel, who worked as a maid between acting jobs, won the part of the family maid Mammy at the Tara plantation.

Selznick cast British actress Vivien Leigh as Southern belle Scarlett O'Hara and matinee idol Clark Gable as Scarlett's suitor, Rhett Butler.

The producer faced criticism from the NAACP and Black newspapers over the racism in Mitchell's book, which romanticizes slavery.

Earl Morris of the Pittsburgh Courier, a Black newspaper, predicted that "Gone With the Wind" would be even more racist than the movie "The Birth of a Nation." Selznick studio officials responded to Morris, telling him that the n-word had been deleted from the movie's script and agreeing to exclude the book's references to the Ku Klux Klan.

The film premiered in racially segregated Atlanta on Dec. 15, 1939. An estimated 300,000 people lined the street to see the movie's stars in a parade. Guests at the Loews Grand Theater included elderly Confederate War veterans. Also performing was a choir of African American children, including 10-year-old Martin Luther King Jr.

When the nearly four-hour movie ended, Atlanta Mayor William Hartsfield spoke. "His voice shook as he called upon the members of the cast and thanked them," the New York Times reported. "He asked the audience to applaud the Negro members of the cast, none of whom was present." McDaniel had declined to attend because she couldn't sit in the theater or stay at the same hotels as White cast members.

The Chicago Defender, a Black newspaper, called the movie a "weapon of terror against Black America." Most newspapers gave the film rave reviews, and many singled out McDaniel for praise. "No one who sees the picture can ever forget her," the Atlanta Constitution reviewer wrote. "In fact, she stole the show quite frequently."

In early 1940, McDaniel was nominated for an Oscar. She attended the awards ceremony as a special guest of Selznick because the Ambassador Hotel didn't typically allow African Americans. She and her escort, Black actor Ferdinand Yober, and her White agent sat at a small table at the back of the ballroom, behind a long table for the movie's White cast members.

FIGURE 15: HATTIE MCDANIEL

The ceremony, like current ones, dragged into the night. Columnist Harold Heffernan described what happened next: "It was 12:50 a.m.— nearly five hours after the starting bell — before the twelfth annual Academy Awards dinner managed to whip up a flicker of excitement. Then — with only a pair of statues to best supporting actor and actress left — the drooping dinner came to life."

Actress Fay Bainter announced the award for best supporting actress. "Spectators stifled their yawns and leaned forward expectantly — then gasped. ... For Miss Bainter had called for Hattie McDaniel" to receive the award, the columnist wrote. "There was silence for several moments, and then the tumult got under way. ...The crowd was tendering an ovation never paralleled in Academy history."

McDaniel gave a short and emotional acceptance speech. "I sincerely hope that I shall always be a credit to my race and the motion picture industry," she concluded, and left the stage in tears. "Gone With the Wind" won eight of the 20 awards, including best picture and best actress.

Hollywood columnist Louella Parsons hailed McDaniel's award as a breakthrough showing "race or color must not interfere where credit is due." Columnist

Jimmie Fidler took a different view: "And where does this Negro artist go from here? Why back to playing incidental comedy maids, of course. I don't think it will be easy for me to laugh at Hattie's comedy in the future."

Fidler was right. McDaniel continued to be offered roles mainly as maids and cooks. The NAACP's executive director, Walter White, singled her out in criticizing Black actors playing subservient and stereotypical parts. McDaniel responded, "I would rather make $700 a week playing a maid than $7 being one."

In 1947, McDaniel landed the title role of the popular national radio program "The Beulah Show," again portraying a comic maid. A few years later, she was diagnosed with breast cancer. She died in 1952 at age 57.

The actress faced racism even in death. She had asked to be buried in Hollywood Cemetery, but the cemetery was closed to African Americans. In October 1952, 3,000 people attended McDaniel's funeral in Los Angeles. "After the funeral services, 125 limousines formed a procession to Rosedale Cemetery, where she was buried," the New York Times reported.

When McDaniel died, her estate was valued at about $10,000, equal to $106,000 now. Most of it went to paying back taxes. She willed $1 to one of her four ex-husbands. She bequeathed her Oscar to Howard University in Washington, D.C., but it has been lost.

In recent years, "Gone With the Wind" has faced a backlash because of its racism, but adjusted for inflation it is still the highest-grossing film ever. McDaniel's reputation has risen as a Black movie pioneer who had little power to choose her roles.

In 2010, when Black actress Mo'Nique accepted the Oscar for best supporting actress for her role in "Precious," she wore white gardenias, as McDaniel had 70 years before. "I want to thank Miss Hattie McDaniel," Mo'Nique said, "for enduring all she had to, so I would not have to."

# CHAPTER 16

# THE MARKETING OF MARILYN MONROE

By Ronald G. Shafer
*This article was first published in The Washington Post on September 24, 2022*

"MARILYN MONROE DIES; PILLS BLAMED"

That was the front-page headline on an Aug. 6, 1962, Los Angeles Times story that began, "Marilyn Monroe, a troubled beauty who failed to find happiness as Hollywood's brightest star, was discovered dead in her Brentwood home of an apparent overdose of sleeping pills Sunday."

More than 60 years after her death at age 36, the "blonde bombshell" is as much of a sensation as she ever was.

The longevity is fueled in part by bizarre speculation that the actress was murdered, with suspects ranging from the Kennedys and the CIA to Teamsters union leader Jimmy Hoffa and the Mafia. But mainly Marilyn Monroe's sex appeal has lasting commercial appeal, as capsulized by a 1973 headline in the Ithaca (N.Y.) Journal: "MM: Still Making Money."

Just this year, Andy Warhol's silk-screen portrait "Shot Sage Blue Marilyn" sold for more than $195 million at Christie's, a record for a 20th-century artwork sold at auction. On Wednesday, Netflix will release a widely anticipated film about Monroe, "Blonde," based on a 2000 novel of the same name by Joyce Carol Oates. The closest equivalence to the Marilyn phenomenon is the adulation for Britain's Princess Diana 25 years after she died in a car crash.

Monroe never was nominated for an Academy Award, but she was the most famous actress in the world. She grew up as Norma Jeane Mortenson (and later Norma Jeane Baker) in Los Angeles-area orphanages and foster homes. She dropped out of high school and soon became a photo model, first as a brunette then as a bleached blonde. In 1946, at age 20, she signed a movie contract with 20th

Century Fox, which changed her name to Marilyn Monroe. (Monroe was the maiden name of her mother, who was in a mental institution.)

By 1953, the curvaceous actress was a worldwide sex symbol, starring in the musical comedies "Gentlemen Prefer Blondes" and "How to Marry a Millionaire." Already others were cashing in on her fame. In December 1953, Hugh Hefner published his first Playboy magazine with a photo of Monroe on the cover and a calendar photo inside of a nude Marilyn against a red velvet curtain. Hefner paid a photographer $500 for the calendar photo, equal to about $5,500 today. Monroe was paid nothing. "I never even received a thank-you from all those who made millions off a nude Marilyn photograph," she said, according to the 1995 book "Marilyn: Her Life in Her Own Words" by photographer George Barris.

Monroe's private life was less successful. In 1942, at age 16, she married the boy next door; they divorced four years later. In 1954, she wed retired New York Yankees star Joe DiMaggio and divorced him nine months later. Her 1956 marriage to playwright Arthur Miller ended in divorce in 1961.

That year, Monroe became enamored with new President John F. Kennedy, and the feeling was mutual. According to numerous biographies, they spent a night together at the Palm Springs, Calif., home of singer Bing Crosby. In May 1962, the actress created a sensation at Madison Square Garden when she sang a sultry "Happy Birthday" to Kennedy while wearing a dress so tight it had to be sewed on. "I can now retire from politics," JFK quipped. (This year, Kim Kardashian caused a stir at a Metropolitan Museum of Art gala by wearing the Monroe dress, which she borrowed from Ripley's Believe It or Not museum. Ripley's purchased the dress in 2016 for $4.8 million.)

FIGURE 16: MARILYN MONROE

By early 1962, Monroe had begun taking prescription drugs to cope with anxiety. In June, 20th Century Fox suspended her from the filming of "Something's Got to Give" after she kept missing work. She stayed secluded in her Spanish-style home in the Brentwood section of Los Angeles. That's where, in the early morning of Aug. 5, her psychiatrist found the dead actress "nude, lying face down on her bed clutching a telephone receiver in her hand," an empty pill bottle nearby, the Los Angeles Times reported. The county coroner ruled her death "a probable suicide."

Monroe was buried in a crypt in Westwood Village Memorial Park in Los Angeles. But her legend lived on. In 1973, Newsday reported a "resurgence of interest" in Monroe. "By mid-October the shelves of department stores and gift shops throughout the country will be stocked with Marilyn Monroe jigsaw puzzles," playing cards, date books and calendars, Newsday wrote, adding, "From Paris came word that 'the Marilyn Monroe look' — tight skirts, tight sweaters, high heels — is back in vogue." Said a former Monroe publicist: "Everyone who can make a buck off Marilyn's memory is trying to do it."

Everybody from Monroe's housekeeper to novelist Norman Mailer wrote books about the star. In his best-selling 1973 book, "Marilyn: A Biography,"

Mailer included previously published claims that Monroe had an affair with married Attorney General Robert F. Kennedy and was murdered by the CIA. In a TV interview with Mike Wallace, Mailer admitted he didn't believe the speculation but included it to sell books because "I needed money very badly."

By 1982, Monroe was more popular than ever, the Associated Press reported. That year, she appeared on the cover of Life magazine for the 19th time, more than any other movie star. "Monroe's estate is still earning thousands of dollars by licensing the late Hollywood star's image," the AP reported, noting that an opera titled "Marilyn" was "among the most successful attractions in Italy during the 1982 season."

Monroe murder theories continued to surface that year. One was that Teamsters leader Hoffa had the actress killed out of revenge for Robert Kennedy's investigations of him. Los Angeles County District Attorney John Van de Kamp ordered a new autopsy on Monroe's body. His office concluded there was "no credible evidence supporting a murder theory." Van de Kamp expressed "the faint hope that Marilyn Monroe be permitted to rest in peace."

But the rumors raged on. A 2017 documentary, "Unacknowledged," claimed Monroe was murdered because she threatened to reveal classified information proving the existence of space aliens.

The Monroe legend has thrived mainly on her made-in-Hollywood sex image. "Forty years after her death," the Hartford Courant reported in 2002, "Monroe is still Hollywood's most successful invention, its most instantly recognized product." When Playboy founder Hefner died in 2017, he was buried at Westwood cemetery next to Monroe in a crypt he had purchased in 1992 for $75,000, about $160,000 now. Hefner had said, "Spending eternity next to Marilyn is too sweet to pass up," the Los Angeles Times reported.

More than a dozen films have been made about Monroe. Netflix promotes its new movie "Blonde," starring Ana de Armas, as "a boldly reimagined fictional portrait" of the Hollywood legend. The movie is rated NC-17 because of graphic "sexual content." Despite her sex-symbol image, Monroe's films rarely ventured beyond what today would be PG-13 territory. In a 1962 interview, she expressed surprise she could show her navel in a movie for the first time in "Something's Got to Give." "I guess the censors are willing to recognize that everyone has a navel," she said.

Six decades after her death, Monroe's image still rakes in big box-office dollars. Yet the real-life Monroe remains mysterious. In the book by photographer Barris, she is quoted as saying two months before her death: "I'm not the girl next door — I'm not a goody-goody — but I think I'm human. As far as I'm concerned, the happiest time of my life is now. There's a future, and I can't wait to get to it. It should be interesting."

# SECTION 4

# PONIES, PLANES
AND AUTOMOBILES

# CHAPTER 17

# THE PONY EXPRESS SCANDAL

By Ronald G. Shafer
*This article was first published in The Washington Post on August 10, 2022*

At about 9 p.m. on a Saturday in late December 1860, Interior Secretary Jacob Thompson rushed to his department's Washington D.C. headquarters to inspect a safe that held bonds and stocks for Native American tribes. The safe key was missing. So Thompson sent for a blacksmith, who smashed the iron safe open with a sledgehammer.

Thompson had heard that hundreds of thousands of dollars in stocks and bonds had been secretly removed and "loaned" to an unknown official. To his shock, the securities were indeed missing from the safe. The recipient turned out to be the president of the Pony Express, who had used the bonds to raise operating money for the private mail service.

The search didn't rise to the level of this week's announcement by former president Donald Trump that his home and safe at his Mar-a-Lago Club in Palm Springs, Fla., had been raided by FBI agents. But it was big news in its day. "Washington City yesterday was thrown into a high state of excitement" by the news that the Interior Department "had been robbed of a very large amount of stocks and bonds held in trust for the benefit of different Indian tribes," the New York Herald reported.

The Justice Department and FBI haven't revealed what the agents were looking for at Mar-a-Lago, but the search required approval by a federal judge. The 1860 break-in was anything but authorized — an inglorious chapter in the legendary Pony Express's horseback transport of mail across the northern plains of America's wild west in the months leading up to the Civil War.

In early 1860, Pony Express President William H. Russell and two business partners created the Central Overland California & Pikes Peak Express Co., following protests over the postmaster general's cuts in mail service to California. At that time, mail trains and telegraph service to the west ended in St. Joseph, Mo. Stagecoaches then carried the telegrams to a station in northern California and the mail on to San Francisco. The trip took up to three weeks.

The new company promised mail delivery by its Pony Express service in 10 days using relays of riders and fast horses. The company bought 400 horses and hired 80 riders. Mark Twain wrote that "the pony-rider was usually a little bit of a man, brimful of spirit and endurance."

Riders traveled light, carrying only a specially designed mail pouch called a mochila, a Bible and a revolver. They were paid about $100 a month, equal to nearly $3,200 now. The most famous rider was a young William "Buffalo Bill" Cody.

The first rider left from St. Joseph on April 3, 1860. A large crowd gathered "to witness the inauguration of this great and novel enterprise," the New York Times reported. At 7:15 p.m., the rider's "spirited bay mare … dashed off at a rapid rate, bearing her burden towards the Gold State." The rider carried 49 letters, five telegrams, newspapers and other items. Ten days later, crowds lined the streets in Sacramento to witness the arrival of the Pony Express rider just after 5 p.m., as church and fire engine bells rang.

To promote the service, the Pony Express made an "extra" run in November to deliver the results of the 1860 presidential election to the West Coast in a record seven days from the new end of the telegraph line in Fort Kearney, Neb. The "Pony" delivered the news that Republican Abraham Lincoln had won New York state and was assured of election.

The federal government partially subsidized the Pony Express route, but the company wasn't able to get the major mail contract. Behind the scenes, the Pony Express was losing money hand over hoof. Russell desperately began seeking ways to pay off creditors.

FIGURE 17: THE 1960 PONY EXPRESS STAMP

He turned first to the War Department, which owed the Pony Express's parent company money for transporting military supplies. Congress hadn't appropriated the funds yet, but War Secretary John Floyd illegally gave Russell and his partners a written assurance of future payment. Russell used the document as collateral to get short-term bank loans. Now the loans were coming due.

Then Russell learned about an Interior Department clerk named Godard Bailey, who was the custodian of a fund that made payments to Native American tribes for land sold to the U.S. government. Bailey was related to Floyd by marriage and worried that Floyd's illegal assurance would be exposed if he didn't help Russell. So he gave Russell bonds and stocks worth about $870,000, or $29 million today. Russell pretended the securities were his and used them to raise cash.

In December, the guilt-ridden Bailey wrote a letter to a friend confessing his theft. On hearing of the letter, Thompson raced to his agency and discovered the bonds were missing. A search of agency books went on "with members of the Cabinet and other prominent public men until three in the morning," the New York Herald reported.

That same morning, federal authorities issued a warrant for Bailey's arrest. "He attempted to cut his throat, but was prevented by his wife," the Chicago Tribune reported. On Christmas Eve, Russell was arrested at his office in New York City.

The story of the Great Bond Robbery quickly became a newspaper sensation. In April, Russell resigned under pressure as Pony Express president. Floyd also resigned his Cabinet position under President James Buchanan because of the scandal and disclosures that he was siphoning federal supplies to Southern rebels. After the Civil War broke out on April 12, 1861, Floyd, a former Virginia governor, became a Confederate general. (Thompson, who had served as a congressman from Mississippi, also quit his post in the Buchanan administration in 1861 to become inspector general of the Confederate Army.)

Meanwhile, the rising tensions between the North and South boosted the Pony Express's business, as people on the West Coast were anxious for timely news about the crisis. But the Pony's days were numbered. On Oct. 26, the opening of a telegraph station in Salt Lake City established nearly nationwide service.

Two days later, the Pony Express company announced it was closing. Soon afterward, the last rider to California journeyed into the sunset. Over the 18 months the Pony Express existed, four riders were killed by Indians, one was hanged for murder, two froze to death and one was killed in an unrelated accident, according to the National Park Service.

With the Civil War underway, the missing bonds were never recovered. Russell and Bailey were never prosecuted. Eventually, U.S. taxpayers footed the bill for replenishing the Indian Trust Fund.

# CHAPTER 18

# DID THE WRIGHT BROTHERS INVENT THE AIRPLANE?

By Ronald G. Shafer
*This article was first published in The Washington Post on December 11, 2021*

The label on the aircraft displayed at the Smithsonian Institution in Washington, D.C., read: "The first man-carrying aeroplane in the history of the world capable of sustained free flight. Invented, built and tested over the Potomac River by Samuel Pierpont Langley in 1903."

Wait. Didn't the brothers Orville and Wilbur Wright invent the airplane?

That's what an angry Orville Wright, the surviving Wright brother, protested in 1925. The label, put on display a few years earlier, set off a nearly 20-year feud between the Smithsonian and Wright. The dispute's roots went back to the very birth of flight.

In late 1903, the Wright brothers and Langley, the Smithsonian's director, were racing to be the first to fly a powered aircraft. The 69-year-old Langley, an astronomer and inventor financed by federal funding equal to $1.6 million today, worked out of a spacious laboratory in the Smithsonian Castle on Washington's National Mall. The Wrights, operating on a shoestring budget, labored in their bicycle shop in Dayton, Ohio, and a field in North Carolina. Both brothers were in their 30s.

Langley was first to try to get his flying machine off the ground. The machine, called "The Buzzard" (and also referred to as the Aerodrome A), was 60 feet long with two 48-foot wings. The plan was to catapult the plane into the air from a houseboat on the Potomac River near Widewater, in Stafford County, Va.

On Oct. 7 at 12:15 p.m., the machine was launched with Langley's assistant aboard. The "mechanical bird ... took the air fairly well," the Washington Star reported. "The next instant the big and curious thing turned gradually downward."

Then "all was wreck and ruin." The aerodrome crashed into the Potomac, a hundred yards from the houseboat.

This "would not in any sense be termed a 'flight,'" the Star concluded.

Langley tried again on Dec. 8 on the Potomac in Washington. A large crowd turned out to watch the history-making event. This time, on launch, the machine did "a half double somersault" and crashed into the water "broken and twisted into a mass of wood, steel and linen, with its nose in the mud on the river bottom," the Star reported. The press dubbed the machine "Langley's Folly."

Then, on Dec. 17, Wilbur Wright and his younger brother, Orville, tested their flying machine, the Wright Flyer, in a field in Kill Devil Hills near Kitty Hawk, N.C. It was a biplane with a rudder in the middle over a gasoline engine. Orville, who weighed less than 150 pounds, was at the controls, lying flat on his stomach.

The plane taxied, lifted off and "soon had attained a height of 60 feet above the rolling sand dunes," the Dayton Daily News reported. The plane flew against a 27-mile-per-hour wind "without difficulty and maintained an average speed of eight miles an hour with ease."

A "small crowd of fish folks and coast guards" followed beneath the plane "with exclamations of wonder, but it soon drew away from them," the paper said. Soon Orville "let his machine alight as easily and as gracefully as a bird."

The plane had flown for 12 seconds and a distance of 120 feet. It was the first successful airplane flight in history. The brothers flew their invention three more times. The longest flight was 59 seconds and 852 feet, with Wilbur at the controls. Afterward, Orville wired back to Dayton: "Success: Will be home for Christmas."

FIGURE 18: ORVILLE AND WILBUR WRIGHT

The brothers soon made planes that could fly considerable distances, and they became world-famous celebrities. A photo of Wilbur flying a plane around the Statue of Liberty in 1909 ran on the cover of Harper's Weekly above the headline "A NEW KIND OF GULL IN NEW YORK HARBOR."

Langley died in 1906, some said of a broken heart; Wilbur died six years later of typhoid fever. In 1914, new Smithsonian director Charles Walcott, an old friend of Langley, had Langley's flying machine restored and tested by Glenn Curtiss, a pilot and aviation manufacturer whom the Wrights had sued for patent infringement. (In 1922, a federal appeals court ordered Curtiss to pay the Wrights royalties because their patent covered all controlled flying machines. The companies founded by Curtiss and the Wrights later merged.)

Curtiss concluded that the Langley plane had been capable of flight; the problem had been the catapult. In 1918, the Smithsonian put the restored Buzzard on display at the National Museum, and over the years Walcott revised the label to call Langley's invention the first airplane.

Orville Wright did not take this one lying down. In a 1925 public letter about the Smithsonian's Langley exhibit, Wright asserted that "the machine now hanging in the institution is, much of it, new material and some of it of different construction from the original," and "the card attached to the machine is not true of the original machine or of the restored one."

Wright set off a national firestorm by revealing in his letter that he planned to send the Wright Flyer to the Science Museum at South Kensington in London. "No one could possibly regret more than I do that our machine must go into a foreign museum," he wrote.

The Smithsonian refused to budge. Congress held hearings. Republican Rep. Roy Fitzgerald of Ohio called the institution's stance "an outrage against the Wright brothers and an attempt to cheat them out of the victory of their discoveries."

In 1928, new Smithsonian director Charles Abbot issued a statement offering to revise the offending label, but only "if Mr. Wright will openly state in a friendly way" that "he believes that the Langley machine was capable of flight under its own power." Wright considered the offer an insult and shipped off the Wright Flyer.

Finally, in 1942, the Smithsonian caved under pressure. It reported that Abbot had "tendered sincere apologies to Dr. Orville Wright for misleading statements by former Smithsonian officials," and it said if the Wright plane were sent to the Smithsonian, it would be given "the highest place of honor which is its due."

On Dec. 17, 1943, President Franklin D. Roosevelt announced, "I am glad to be able to tell you that Orville Wright is going to bring the Kitty Hawk plane back from England where it has been in the British Museum. The nation will welcome it back as the outstanding symbol of American genius."

Until the end of World War II, the Wright plane was stored safely in an underground chamber about 100 miles from London. Before the plane could be returned, Orville Wright died of a heart attack in January 1948. He had seen plane speeds go from about 30 miles per hour on his first flight to 662 mph in 1947, when Air Force Capt. Chuck Yeager broke the sound barrier.

The Wright Flyer finally was unveiled at the Smithsonian's Arts and Industries Building on Dec. 17, 1948. Its placard read: "The world's first power-driven, heavier-than-air machine in which man made free-controlled and sustained flight, invented and built by Wilbur and Orville Wright ..."

In 1976, the Wright plane moved to a place of prominence in the new National Air and Space Museum. A century after infuriating Orville Wright with its plaque crediting Langley for inventing the airplane, the Smithsonian is all in on celebrating the Wrights for the accomplishment.

But Langley was ultimately recognized for his research, if not for inventing the airplane. Langley Air Force Base and NASA's Langley Research Center in Hampton, Va., are both named after him.

# CHAPTER 19

# THE FIRST ELECTRIC CARS

By Ronald G. Shafer
*This article was first published in The Washington Post on February 24, 2019*

Long before Elon Musk's Tesla cars, electric automobiles roamed the streets of the nation's capital. President William Howard Taft's wife drove an electric car. President Woodrow Wilson rode in an electric, and his wife drove one.

By the turn of the 20th century, horseless carriages had replaced horse-drawn carriages in most major American cities. In 1901, an estimated 38 percent of cars in the United States were electric, 40 percent were powered by steam, and 22 percent ran on gasoline. As a result, streets were cleaner and less stinky in many cities. In New York City alone, horses had deposited about 2.5 million pounds of manure on the streets every day.

By 1915, Washington had 1,325 electric cars, about the same number as Detroit. This ranked behind Chicago with 4,000 electrics and New York with 3,200. In Washington, "the automotive public has had an awakening and has found that the modern electric car truly is an eye opener," said W.R. Emerson of Emerson & Orma, the local dealership for an Anderson Electric Car Co. model called the Detroit Electric.

Women were the driving force behind electric cars. The electrics were cleaner, quieter and easier to drive than steamers and especially gasoline cars, which spewed smelly fumes and had to be started with a hand crank. Denver socialite Margaret Whitehead drove a Fritsche Electric because, she said, a lady "can wear the most perishable and delicately hued gown she possesses, and the daintiest of footwear without giving a thought, for when she arrives at her destination, she is unsullied and her coiffure is as unruffled as when she left the house."

The first families in Washington also influenced car trends. The 330-pound President Taft preferred to ride in a big, open-top White Model M steam car made by White Motor Co. But in 1909, his wife, Helen, started driving a two-seater Baker Queen Victoria Electric car around Washington. The first lady's car, made by Baker Motor Vehicle Co., had blue upholstery and the U.S. coat of arms painted on the doors.

Mrs. Taft replaced the Baker in 1912 with a new one. One newspaper said: "The use of an electric car by the President's wife will undoubtedly give a great impetus to the electric vehicle business."

President Wilson, who took office in 1913, chose a gasoline Pierce Arrow as the presidential limousine. But Wilson, who never learned how to drive, sometimes rode around Washington in a Milburn Light Electric, made by the Milburn Wagon Co. His Secret Service agents drove Milburns as well.

Both Wilson's first wife, Ellen, who died in 1914, and his second wife, Edith Bolling Galt, drove Helen Taft's Baker Electric. The second Mrs. Wilson, Edith, before marrying the president, was reportedly the first woman to drive an electric car in the District of Columbia, in 1904.

Owners of electric cars charged their vehicles at charging stables, often located at auto dealerships. Electric carmakers, such as Oliver Frichtle in Denver, promoted the distance their cars could go on a single battery charge.

Frichtle was the Elon Musk of his day. Musk has vowed to send a driverless Tesla with autopilot from Los Angeles to New York City. In 1914, Frichtle drove one of his cars from Lincoln, Neb., to the Big Apple, a distance of 1,800 miles, in 29 days. He recharged the battery at charging stations along the way and averaged close to 90 miles per charge.

FIGURE 19: EDITH BOLLING GAIT

Ads for electric cars were published in Washington papers. A 1914 ad boasted that buyers of the Detroit Electric, "Society's Town Car," included inventor Thomas Edison and Henry Ford, who made gasoline cars in Detroit.

Ford bought a Detroit Electric every two years for his wife, Clara. She preferred the cleaner electric cars to the smoke-belching autos her husband produced. Her car had a special child seat for the Fords' son Edsel.

Electric cars improved from early models that "carried a couple tons of storage battery around on four wheels at scarcely better than an overgrown snail's pace," W.C. Anderson, president of Anderson Electric Car Co., said in 1912. "The electric car of today" is "considered up to date," he said. "There's no question that the electric vehicle has a great future."

But Anderson was wrong. Electric cars started losing their appeal after Ford began mass production of his gasoline Model T. In 1912, the Model T sold for $650, compared with $1,750 for a comparable electric car. In today's dollars, the Model T cost $17,000 versus $47,000 for the electric.

Also in 1912, Charles Kettering invented the electric starter for Cadillac, eliminating the need for hand cranks on gasoline cars. Then came the 1920s Texas oil boom, which led to cheap gasoline. Filling stations popped up on roads across the country, bringing gasoline to rural areas that lacked access to electricity needed for electric cars. By the 1930s, electric cars had pretty much faded away.

# SECTION 5

# WALLOWING IN WATERGATE

# CHAPTER 20

# WATCHING THE WATERGATE HEARINGS

By Ronald G. Shafer
*This article was first published in The Washington Post on June 8, 2022*

The hottest TV show in the summer of 1973 was the U.S. Senate's version of the popular quiz show "Truth or Consequences."

In place of Bob Barker, the host was Senate Watergate Committee Chairman Samuel Ervin Jr. (D-N.C.), who grilled witnesses in his folksy style, quipping, "I am just an old country lawyer, and I don't know the finer ways to do it. I just have to do it my way."

Instead of trivia, the participants were asked about their knowledge of the 1972 break-in and phone-bugging at Democratic headquarters in the Watergate office building in D.C. But if the subject matter was a bit more opaque, the ratings were even better.

As the House Select Committee investigating the Jan. 6, 2021, attack on the U.S. Capitol prepares to kick off the first of a series of televised hearings Thursday, some in evening prime time, it's hard to think of a political spectacle more analogous — and TV-worthy — than the Watergate hearings of nearly a half-century ago.

This summer's hearings promise to produce fireworks from the start. "The hearings will tell a story that will really blow the roof off the House," Rep. Jamie B. Raskin (D-Md.) said.

By contrast, when the Watergate hearings began on May 17, 1973, little was known about the Watergate break-in except that five burglars had been arrested, some with ties to President Richard M. Nixon's Committee for Re-Election of the President, known to Nixon critics as CREEP. The first witness was one of the burglars, James McCord Jr., who was CREEP's security chief. His testimony was less-than-riveting TV. "If you like to watch grass grow, you would have loved the opening" of the Watergate hearings, The Washington Post reported.

The drama picked up in June, when former White House counsel John Dean III testified about a Watergate coverup. Dean said he had told Nixon there was "a cancer growing on the presidency."

Among the spectators during Dean's five days of testimony were former Beatle John Lennon and his wife, Yoko Ono. "Since we saw the Watergate hearings on TV, we thought we'd take them in," Lennon said. The plot took a sensational turn on July 16 when a surprise witness, former White House aide Alexander Butterfield, revealed that Nixon had secretly taped his conversations.

By now, all eyes were on the televised hearings. "The Senate Watergate investigation is proving a television-viewing phenomenon," columnist Jack Anderson wrote. A.C. Nielsen reported that an estimated three out of four of the nation's homes watched at least part of the hearings. The drama-filled inquiry outdrew popular daytime soap operas. "I watched the Watergate hearings for three days before I realized it wasn't the 'Secret Storm,' " wrote humor columnist Erma Bombeck.

People tuned in day and night, newspapers reported. A grave digger in Boston took time off during the day to watch the hearings at a bar to get "an education." A Chicago woman told a friend: "I've gotta hurry home and watch the Senate investigation on TV. It's more fun than an X-rated movie." At Washington's upscale Sans Souci restaurant, business was "dragging" during the hearings, its maître d' said, because people "were home watching television."

Chairman Ervin, with his bushy "dancing eyebrows," was an instant TV star. "Thanks to the Watergate hearings, Sen. Sam J. Ervin Jr. is well on his way to becoming an authentic American folk hero," United Press International wrote. "Sam Ervin Fan Clubs are sprouting up all across the land," and there was even a song, "The Ballad of Senator Sam," calling him the "greatest thing since country ham."

FIGURE 20: SEN. SAM ERVIN, WATERGATE COMMITTEE CHAIRMAN

"After 19 years in the Washington phone book," Ervin "got an unlisted home phone number to avoid the press" and admirers, Washington Post columnist Jeanette Smyth wrote. "A Dallas woman wanted to marry the 76-year-old senator."

Ervin's sidekick was Sen. Howard Baker (R-Tenn.), the urbane co-chairman who on July 23, 1973, asked the famous question, "What did the president know, and when did he know it?" Smyth reported, "Baker, 47, leads the hit parade with about 100 mash notes and is said to be embarrassed about it. The notes range from that of a lusty 69-year-old who wrote, 'I could vote for you for President all day and all night, too,' to the cheeky babysitter who penciled, 'You broke my heart Sen. Baker! I was all set on marrying you (so what if you're 30 years older) when I found out you were already married.' "

Ervin and Baker weren't the only committee senators drawing romantic attention. Smyth wrote: "The switchboard at Sen. Edward J. Gurney's (R-Fla.) Northwest Washington apartment building lights up with calls from women wanting to know if the wavy-haired 59-year-old is 'unattached and available.' (He has been married for 33 years.)"

Boyish-looking Dean, 34, with his horn-rimmed glasses and button-down shirt, appealed to women of all ages. "John Dean was a hit, I was told at the beauty parlor," one reporter wrote from Harbor Beach, Mich. Some women called him "clean-cut, regular-featured, soft-spoken, the kind of a fellow a woman would want her son to be, or a girl her beau."

Not everyone involved in the hearings drew such rave reviews. "The best time to go to the bathroom when watching the Watergate hearings," humor columnist

Art Buchwald wrote, is when Sen. Joseph Montoya (D-N.M.) "is questioning the witness."

The three major TV networks rotated live coverage of the hearings. The Public Broadcasting System's audience boomed with its gavel-to-gavel coverage, including taped reruns at night. PBS stations tried pairing fundraising drives with their coverage, with mixed results. "We cleaned up with John Dean" but did "poorly" with dour former attorney general John Mitchell, said a spokeswoman for the PBS outlet in Miami.

Nixon, at an Aug. 22 news conference, downplayed the hearings as "water under the bridge." Republican Senate leader Robert J. Dole of Kansas called for closing down the televised inquiry, contending that "the people want the hearings off the screen." An Ervin spokesman countered that 90 percent of the 14,000 letters the panel had received since Nixon's news conference favored continuing the inquiry.

The hearings went on until November. By the next summer, after the White House released the Nixon tapes under order from the Supreme Court, there was talk of new televised hearings — this time to impeach the president. Nixon pre-empted those by announcing to a nationwide television audience on Aug. 8, 1974, that he was resigning and turning the presidency over to Vice President Gerald Ford. Nixon's announcement drew 110 million viewers, second all-time among non-sports events only to the 1969 moon landing.

Disclosures in the Watergate hearings were widely credited with forcing Nixon's resignation. "The live television Senate Watergate hearings were a gradual course in civics and political science. They're among television's finest hours." CBS newsman Dan Rather wrote in 1973. He added a word of advice that feels newly relevant ahead of the Jan. 6 hearings: "Remember Watergate. Somebody, lest we forget, ravaged the Constitution and very nearly stole the government."

\

# CHAPTER 21

# WHAT'S FUNNY ABOUT WATERGATE

By Ronald G. Shafer
*This article was first published in The Washington Post on June 14, 2022*

"Did you hear about the new Watergate watch? Both hands always point to Nixon."

The Watergate scandal began 50 years ago this month, and so did a golden age of political humor. The jokes started flying soon after five burglars were caught bugging the phones at Democratic National Committee headquarters in the Watergate office building during the 1972 presidential race between Republican President Richard M. Nixon and Democratic Sen. George McGovern of South Dakota.

"McGovern knew something suspicious was going on when he picked up a grapefruit and got a dial tone," quipped Mark Russell, the piano-playing comedian at Washington's Shoreham Hotel.

The humor of Watergate contrasts with the seriousness of the current national focus on the violent attack on the U.S. Capitol on Jan. 6, 2021, by supporters of President Donald Trump, which resulted in the deaths of five people. The attack is under investigation by the Justice Department and a House select committee, whose highly anticipated hearings have been compared to the Watergate hearings.

But the Watergate scandal had overtones of a Keystone Kops comedy. It involved what the Nixon White House called a "third rate" burglary, "inoperative statements," a political coverup and secret presidential recordings that provided plenty of fodder for political satire. "For comedians, Watergate was the gift that kept on giving," said Russell in an email.

The Watergate break-in took place on June 17, 1972. Two days later, young Washington Post reporters Bob Woodward and Carl Bernstein disclosed that some of the burglars worked for Nixon's Committee for Re-Election of the President, known to Nixon critics as CREEP. From then on, you could follow the humor. On June 23, a Post cartoon by Herbert Block, known as Herblock, showed footprints representing the "bugging case" in front of the White House. A detective with a magnifying glass was saying, "Strange—they all seem to have some connection with this place."

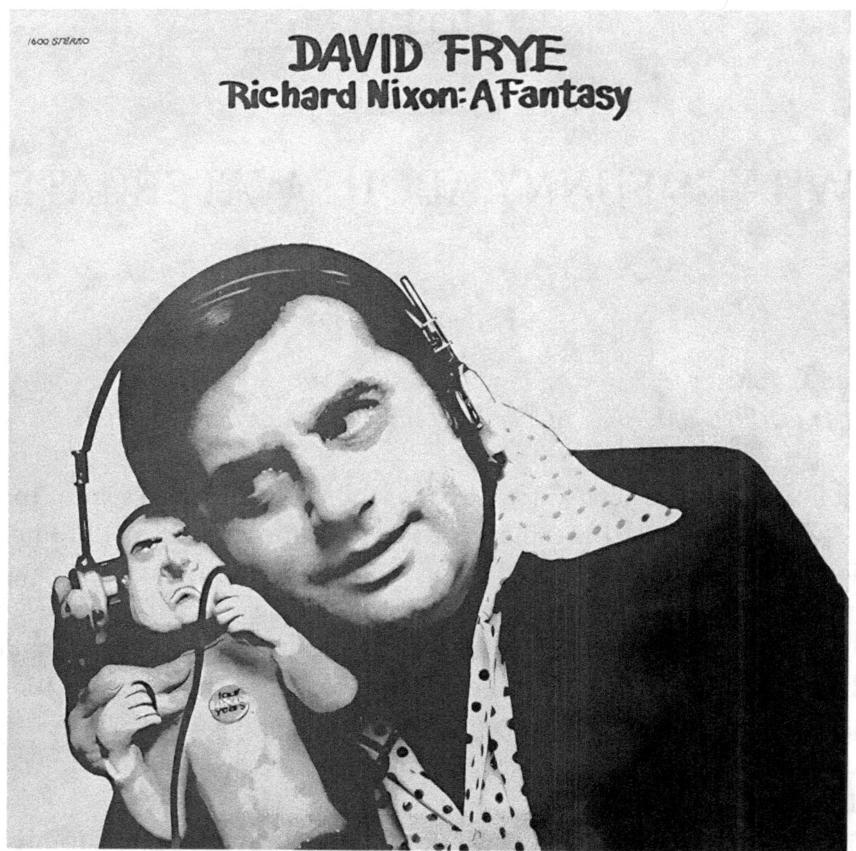


FIGURE 21: COMEDIAN DAVID FRYE

The White House's coverup began to unravel after Nixon won reelection. By mid-1973, comedian David Frye was playing to packed nightclub audiences, impersonating the president as he wallowed in Watergate. "My fellow Americans. There is a bright side to Watergate," said Frye as Nixon. "My administration has taken crime out of the streets and put it in the White House, where I can keep an eye on it."

Frye's Nixon went on: "The odds are 100 to 1 that I'll be impeached, 50 to 1 that I'll resign. That is not the reason that I am today signing a Prison Reform Bill. There will be a two-bedroom suite for anyone who once held the nation's highest office."

At least five Watergate comedy record albums became the hottest-selling political comedy albums since Vaughn Meader made fun of President John F. Kennedy on his album "The First Family" in 1962. On "The Watergate Comedy Hour," a compilation of comic skits, a Nixon impersonator began a prayer, "My fellow God."

Gerald Gardner's "The Watergate Follies" became a best-selling book, with captioned photos such as one showing Nixon talking to reporters with a speech bubble reading, "Are you going to believe me or the facts?" "The Watergate Cookbook" featured recipes such as Watergate Vichyssoise — to start, "Take a bunch of leaks..." There was even a board game called "The Watergate Game." The object was "to stay out of jail."

After the Senate Watergate Committee uncovered the existence of secret White House tapes, there was found to be an 18½-minute gap in a recording of Nixon talking three days after the break-in. All that could be heard was a humming sound. Humor columnist Art Buchwald wrote that the sound actually was the president humming. Nixon had kept this a secret, The Washington Post columnist explained, because "he doesn't want to go down in history as the first American President who was known as a nervous hummer."

"Nixon was my Camelot," Buchwald said later. "Every day was something new. I'd wake up in the morning, see something in the paper like the 18-minute tape gap and write my column so quickly that I'd be on the tennis court by 10 o'clock." The columnist proposed that June 17 be declared national Watergate Day to mark the break-in: "Americans would memorialize this historic event by tapping telephones, spying on their neighbors, using aliases and making inoperative statements."

Even late-night TV comedy king Johnny Carson, who usually avoided politics, began telling Watergate jokes after the White House claimed Nixon's secretary Rose Mary Woods had accidentally erased part of the tape. "Let me put it this way," Carson said. "Would you believe Moses if he had come down with the Eight Commandments?"

TV talk-show host Dick Cavett taped one of his shows from the Senate Watergate Committee hearing room, where he interviewed committee members. "While sitting in that witness chair, I feel guilty," Cavett told co-chairman Sen. Howard H. Baker Jr. (R-Tenn.), who replied, "You're the first one." Nixon apparently was a viewer of Cavett's shows. On the White House tapes, the president is heard asking his staff about Cavett: "Is there any way we can screw him?"

As transcripts of the tapes further incriminated Nixon in 1974, a Herblock cartoon showed the president hanging in midair, clinging to two torn pieces of a reel-to-reel tape with the words, "I am not a crook." In late July, the Supreme Court ordered that the tapes be turned over to the Watergate special counsel.

That month, the House Judiciary Committee voted for articles of impeachment charging Nixon with obstruction of justice. Bumper stickers appeared reading, "Honk if you think he's guilty." One political button declared "Jail to the Chief." A joke made the rounds: "The Rev. Billy Graham's Bible readings at the White House have gone from Revelations to Exodus."

On Aug. 9, 1974, Nixon became the only president ever to resign from office and turned the presidency over to Vice President Gerald Ford. A restaurant in suburban Detroit, the New York Times reported, began promoting a "Watergate Special" pizza: "First you order a Richard Nixon. Then you turn on the heat and get a Jerry Ford."

After Nixon left, the Watergate spigot of humor abruptly shut off. "When Watergate was over," said Russell, the pianist-comedian, "I had to go back to writing my own material."

# SECTION 6

# HERE COME THE BRIDES

# CHAPTER 22

# WHITE HOUSE WEDDING

By Ronald G. Shafer
*This article was first published in The Washington Post on February 14, 2019*

A Marine Band orchestra, under the direction of John Philip Sousa, played "The Wedding March" as President Grover Cleveland and his young bride walked arm in arm into the Blue Room. At 7:30 p.m. on June 2, 1886, Cleveland became the first — and only — U.S. president to be married in the White House.

Cleveland, a New York Democrat, is one of three presidents to marry while in office. The first was Virginia's John Tyler, a Whig, in 1844, and the third was Democrat Woodrow Wilson of Virginia in 1915. Cleveland's Valentine love story has several quirky twists.

The 300-pound Cleveland was a bachelor when he moved into the White House in early 1885. He won election despite a sex scandal. During the campaign, a Buffalo newspaper revealed that Cleveland had fathered a child with a single woman named Maria Halpern. A popular cartoon pictured Cleveland and a woman holding a crying baby with the caption: 'Ma, Ma. Where's My Pa?" After Cleveland won, his backers responded, "Gone to the White House. Ha, Ha, Ha."

Rumors that the bachelor president would marry began soon after he took office. Cleveland was close to the family of his late friend, Oscar Folsom, who died in 1873. Folsom left behind his wife, Emma, and their 11-year-old daughter, Frances. Cleveland doted on the daughter, whom he had known since she was born. He called her "Frank," and she called him "Uncle Cleve."

Newspapers speculated that the 44-year-old widow Emma Folsom would be the next first lady. But Cleveland told a friend, "I don't see why the papers keep marrying me to old ladies all the while. I wonder why they don't say I'm engaged to marry her daughter?" The 48-year-old president had, in fact, secretly proposed to

20-year-old Frances in a letter just before she graduated from Wells College in New York in spring 1885.

Soon newspapers began reporting rumors that "Frankie" was the "bride-elect." The Boston Globe printed a long story with a picture of Folsom and the headline "Danced On 'Uncle Cleve's' Knee In Infancy."

Finally on May 28, 1886, the president published their wedding announcement. He planned a small ceremony with about two dozen guests. Cleveland barred the press, but some reporters climbed trees outside the Blue Room to get a view. The wedding was front-page news across the country.

"The bride wore an enchanting wedding dress of ivory," one paper reported.

Frances was ahead of her time and eliminated the word "obey" from her wedding vows. Cleveland didn't kiss the bride. But he gave her an "elegant diamond necklace, the stones being set in gold and extending all around the neck." The wedding cake was a fruitcake

The happy couple soon rode a Baltimore & Ohio train to a private cabin near Deer Park, Md. Reporters followed them and used binoculars to spy on the newlyweds. Cleveland was so furious that he wrote one New York editor that his reporters were "doing their utmost to make American journalism contemptible in the estimation of people of good breeding everywhere."

FIGURE 22: PRESIDENT GROVER CLEVELAND'S WEDDING

Most Americans didn't make a fuss about the age gap between the 49-year-old president and his 21-year-old bride. Folsom still is the youngest first lady ever and then was the most popular since Dolley Madison. Women followed the "Cleveland fashion" in clothes. Companies sold unauthorized "Frankie" products ranging from sewing kits to a tobacco pipe and liver pills.

To maintain some privacy, Cleveland bought a farmhouse on 27 acres in Northwest Washington to use as their primary home. The area later became known as Cleveland Park. The couple soon had their first child, baby Ruth. But in the 1888 presidential race, Cleveland lost to Indiana's Benjamin Harrison. Cleveland won a 1892 rematch and became the only president to serve two nonconsecutive terms.

Back in the White House, the Clevelands had two more daughters. After a second term, the first couple moved to Princeton, N.J., and had a son and another girl. Cleveland died there in 1908 at age 71. Mrs. Cleveland remarried in 1913. But after she died in 1947 at age 83, she was buried with her first love, President Cleveland.

The first sitting president to wed, Tyler, was known as "His Accidency." He moved up from vice president in early 1841 when William Henry "Old Tippecanoe" Harrison became the first president to die in office. In 1842, Tyler's invalid wife, Letitia, also died. The 51-year-old Tyler soon fell in love with 22-year-old Julia Gardiner, the daughter of a wealthy couple from Long Island, N.Y. When a friend told Tyler he might be too old to marry Julia, Tyler replied, "Pooh. Why, my dear sir, I am just full in my prime."

The couple wed on June 26, 1844 in New York City. They were married for nearly 18 years until Tyler died in early 1862. Julia died 27 years later. Tyler set a record unlikely ever to be broken: most children by a president, at 15 (eight with his first wife and seven with Gardiner).

Woodrow Wilson became the third president to marry while in office on Dec. 18, 1915, just a year after his first wife, Ellen, had died of kidney disease. The 59-year-old Wilson fell for 43-year-old Edith Bolling Galt, a wealthy D.C. widow.

The couple were married in a small private wedding at Galt's Washington home. When Wilson suffered a stroke in his second term, Mrs. Wilson secretly took over many presidential duties. After Wilson left office, the couple bought a house near Embassy Row in Northwest Washington. Wilson died there in 1924 at age 67. Mrs. Wilson lived in the house until 1961, when she died at age 89.

The Woodrow Wilson House is now open to the public. In 2015, the house presented a 100-year wedding anniversary exhibit. Among the items: a century-old piece of the Wilsons' wedding plum cake.

# CHAPTER 23

# ALICE ROOSEVELT'S WEDDING CAKE

By Ronald G. Shafer
*This article was first published in The Washington Post on November 19, 2022*

At her White House wedding in 1906, Alice Lee Roosevelt, the lively daughter of Republican President Theodore Roosevelt, grabbed a military guard's sword and sliced her wedding cake in half. "Let somebody else do the rest," she said with a laugh.

On Nov. 19, President Biden's eldest granddaughter will be married in the 19th White House wedding. The nuptials of Naomi Biden and Peter Neal on the South Lawn will probably be less raucous than the early-20th-century matching of "Princess Alice" and Rep. Nicholas Longworth (R-Ohio).

The high-spirited Alice was a handful when Roosevelt, the vice president, moved into the White House in 1901 after President William McKinley was assassinated. "I can do one of two things," Roosevelt told a visitor. "I can be president of the United States, or I can control Alice. I cannot possibly do both!"

Alice loved to ride in fast cars, ride fast horses — and bet on racehorses with bookies — and sneak a smoke on the White House roof. She carried a pet garter snake named Emily Spinach in her purse. In 1903, she rode in a submarine in Narragansett Bay, two years before her father became the first president to go underwater in a sub.

She is "more than a fair portrait and landscape painter ... speaks several languages" and "is fond of poetry, favoring Keats and Shelly," a columnist wrote in 1905. The columnist said that a member of the snooty Knickerbocker Club in New York "after seeing the zest with which she danced, remarked in his languid way, 'Bah, Jove! She is a chip off the old block.' "

FIGURE 23: ALICE ROOSEVELT

Alice became a worldwide celebrity. In 1905, Roosevelt sent his daughter on a diplomatic voyage to the Far East with War Secretary William Howard Taft. The congressional delegation included Longworth, a wealthy playboy. He and Alice began a romance at sea. "One morning Congressman Longworth, Miss Alice's devoted slave, presented himself attired in white flannels," the New York World reported. Alice dared him to jump into the ship's pool, then dived in herself, fully clothed. "What could poor Longworth do, flannels and all but gallantly follow the President's daughter?" the paper recorded.

Alice later wrote that Longworth wasn't the man in flannels, but in any case, that December, she and Longworth announced their engagement. Their wedding was set for Feb. 17, five days after Alice's 22nd birthday. Longworth was 36. It would be the first White House wedding since 1874, when President Ulysses S. Grant's daughter Nellie married Algernon Charles Frederick Sartoris, a prominent Englishman.

Washington was abuzz as the wedding neared. "This is 'Alice Roosevelt week,'" the National Tribune reported. "Nobody in this town who pretends to be anybody is going to think of anything else but going to the White House wedding. Not since pretty Nellie Grant married her foreign lover against her father's wishes in the big East Room of the White House has there been as much interest manifested in a wedding in the United States."

On Feb. 17, crowds of spectators gathered outside the White House gates to get a peek at the wedding guests. The guests included Nellie Grant Sartoris, Supreme Court justices, congressmen, diplomats and Alice's cousin, future president Franklin D. Roosevelt. FDR's wife, Alice's first cousin Eleanor, was pregnant and stayed home.

At noon, Alice, wearing a long white satin dress, marched up the aisle in the East Room on the arm of President Roosevelt. After vows were exchanged, the bride "tripped down from the altar like a school girl, and in the exuberance of her mood almost danced her way through the assemblage of nearly a thousand admiring men and women," reported The Washington Post, which devoted its entire front page to the wedding.

"Alice adorned herself with the pearl necklace from the Cuban government, a diamond broach from her parents, the kaiser's diamond bracelets, and Nick's wedding present to her, a diamond and pearl necklace," Stacy A. Cordery wrote in her book, "Alice."

The bride and groom retreated to the Blue Room for a private lunch with friends. When the big wedding cake was served, Alice exclaimed to the military guard, "Your sword, Major, your sword." Drawing his sword, the guard "grasped the blade and thrust the pearl mounted hilt in the bride's direction," the Hartford Courant reported. "Without any hesitation, she took the weapon firm in her right hand and with one sharp thrust of the point into the centre of the cake cut deep into it. Then deftly drawing the sword hilt downward, she divided it."

About 4 p.m., the newlyweds and some friends slipped out of a window in the Red Room to avoid the waiting crowd. A limousine was waiting to whisk the couple to the nearby estate of Washington Post Publisher John R. McLean. "Showers of rice" were thrown by "the jolly young people who had been skylarking the afternoon away in the White House," the New York Times reported.

Most of the public loved the wedding. But a Chicago pastor called it "a vain display of would-be royalty. ... 'Princess Alice,' who is nothing more nor less than a plain American girl, outdid any of the efforts of Queen Victoria."

The marriage soon became strained. Longworth continued his womanizing. Once, a fellow congressman ran his hand over Longworth's bald head and said, "Nice and smooth. Feels just like my wife's bottom." Longworth felt his own head and replied, "Yes, so it does."

Alice also had affairs. In 1925, at age 41, she gave birth to a daughter, Paulina. The father was married Sen. William Borah (R-Idaho), Alice wrote in her private diary. Longworth doted on Paulina until his death in 1931 at age 61. He had become a popular House speaker, and in 1962, a House office building was named after him.

"Mrs. L." became known for her tart tongue. After telling bawdy jokes about President Woodrow Wilson, she was banned from the White House. She called President Warren G. Harding "just a slob." She said "the Hoover vacuum is more exciting" than President Herbert Hoover but supported him against cousin Franklin D. Roosevelt in the 1932 presidential election. Still, Alice often visited the White House during FDR's four terms. According to the syndicated column Capital Stuff, she once said Roosevelt was "one part mush and two parts Eleanor."

She liked Democratic presidents Harry S. Truman and John F. Kennedy and reportedly voted for Lyndon B. Johnson, but her favorite was Republican Richard M. Nixon, who hosted her 87th birthday party at the White House. In 1971, she attended the White House wedding of Tricia Nixon and Edward Finch Cox.

Mrs. L. never remarried. She presided over Washington society from her home on Embassy Row and became known as the capital's "other Washington Monument." A pillow in her sitting room was embroidered with a saying she popularized: "If you haven't got anything nice to say about anyone, come and sit here by me."

In 1974, she told The Post, "I don't think I am insensitive or cruel. I laugh, I have a sense of humor, I like to tease. I must admit a sense of mischief does get hold of me from time to time. ... Isn't it strange how that upsets people?"

Alice Roosevelt Longworth died Feb. 20, 1980, at age 96. United Press International noted that her wedding nearly seven decades before was "one of the prime social events of the century's first decade."

# SECTION 7

# THE PRESIDENTS

# CHAPTER 24

# JOHN ADAMS VS THOMAS JEFFERSON

By Ronald G. Shafer
*This article was first published in The Washington Post on July 31, 2023*

The vice president of the United States was running against the president he was serving under, and his backers didn't mince words. They accused the president of having a "hideous hermaphroditical character, which has neither the force and firmness of a man, nor the gentleness and sensibility of a woman."

The president's backers fired back, warning that if the vice president won the election, "Murder, robbery, rape, adultery, and incest will be openly taught and practiced."

That vice president, Thomas Jefferson, had once been friends with President John Adams before their 1800 campaign. But the two Founding Fathers had a nasty falling-out — like former vice president Mike Pence did with his now-opponent for the 2024 Republican nomination, former president Donald Trump.

Pence, whose super PAC called Trump "an apologist for thugs and dictators" in a recent ad, is the third veep to run against his former boss and the first since a disastrous challenge in 1940.

Jefferson had become vice president because he had finished second to Adams in 1796, in America's first contested presidential election. The Sage of Monticello differed with Adams's policies, especially on the 1798 Alien and Sedition Acts that made it illegal to criticize the government. In 1800, neither man campaigned personally but spread their views instead through partisan newspapers and pamphlet.

Jeffersonians charged that Federalist Adams was "a monarchist" who had become cozy with the British. Newspapers referred to the portly president as "His Rotundity." Long before Twitter, Jefferson backers spread a conspiracy theory that Adams planned to create a family dynasty by having one of his sons marry one of King George III's daughters. The secret plot, according to the story, was thwarted when George Washington himself, dressed in his Revolutionary War uniform, "had drawn his sword and threatened to run the president through," Ralph A. Brown wrote in "The Presidency of John Adams."

FIGURE 24: JOHN ADAMS

FIGURE 25: THOMAS JEFFERSON

Jefferson paid journalist James Callender to attack Adams in print. Callender, who was out for revenge after being sentenced to prison for violating the Sedition Acts, wrote that "the reign of Mr. Adams has, hitherto, been one of continued tempest of malignant passions." He wrote a false story that Adams wanted to invade France in the aftermath of the French Revolution. Jefferson's party also obtained and leaked to the press a private letter by Treasury Secretary Alexander Hamilton saying Adams had "great and intrinsic defects in his character."

Federalist newspapers attacked Jefferson in response, accusing him of dodging military service during the Revolutionary War. They called him a "howling atheist" who had become a libertine while serving as U.S. ambassador to France. Yale College president and theologian Timothy Dwight warned that Jefferson would make "our wives and daughters the victims of legal prostitution.

The 16 states ended voting in December 1800, just as John and Abagail Adams were moving into the newly constructed President's House in Washington, D.C. Jefferson edged Adams in the electoral college, 73 votes to 65. But there was a hitch. New Yorker Aaron Burr, presumed to be Jefferson's running mate, received the same number of electoral votes as Jefferson, and some Jefferson opponents said Burr should be president. Under the Constitution, the decision was up to the Federalist-controlled U.S. House, which in February 1801 officially elected Jefferson after 36 ballots.

Adams peacefully turned the government over to Jefferson but resented his vice president, becoming the first of five defeated one-term presidents to skip the inauguration of their successor. After two terms in office, though, Jefferson became pen pals with Adams — until both men died on the same day, July 4, 1826.

History repeated a century later. In December 1939, not expecting Franklin D. Roosevelt to run for an unprecedented third term, Vice President John Nance Garner read a short statement from the front porch of his home in Uvalde, Tex., declaring, "I will accept the nomination for president" in 1940. Garner, 71, declined to answer any questions and headed off on a 10-day hunting trip.

"Cactus Jack" Garner ultimately became famous for saying, in the sanitized version, "The vice presidency is not worth a bucket of warm spit." And in the previous two years, he had broken with Roosevelt on various policies, including his attempt to pack the Supreme Court. Garner also represented a conservative bloc of Southern Democrats who opposed Roosevelt's large-spending "New Deal" programs.

"The rebel yell echoed through the crisp air of this hill country town tonight as a tribute to 'Citizen John Garner,'" the Associated Press reported after his announcement. "There was speculation about the effect Garner's announcement will have on his relation to the President with whom he always has been on a friendly personal terms. ... Few believe that the relations would be outwardly disturbed." Roosevelt, from his estate in Hyde Park, N.Y., "had no comment."

Privately, it was a different story, and the two men's personal terms didn't seem so friendly. Speaking of the hard-drinking Garner, Roosevelt joked to his Cabinet, "I see that the vice president has thrown his bottle — I mean his hat — into the ring," former Labor secretary Harold Ickes wrote.

Suspense about Roosevelt's own plans mounted right up to the 1940 Democratic convention in Chicago. There, on the night of July 16, Sen. Alben W. Barkley of Kentucky read a statement from Roosevelt that the president had no "desire or purpose" to be re-nominated ... unless delegates wanted him. The impact was no surprise.

"No sooner had Barkley finished speaking," the AP reported, than the crowd erupted, shouting, "We want Roosevelt" amid "whistling, yelling and stamping." The convention overwhelmingly nominated Roosevelt, with 946 votes to Garner's 61.

Garner, who opposed a third term for any president, was furious, but kept quiet. Roosevelt picked liberal Agriculture Secretary Henry A. Wallace as his new running mate and, with war in Europe on the horizon, won in a landslide

After the election, Garner went back to his ranch in Texas. There, he intended to "go over his fishing tackle, oil up his gun and settle down to live to 93 at a leisurely pace," the AP reported. He lived to 98 instead.

In 1944, Roosevelt won yet another term, after replacing Wallace with Sen. Harry S Truman of Missouri. This time, Roosevelt's vice president would get his promotion without having to run: Three months after his fourth inauguration, Roosevelt died.

# CHAPTER 25

# LINCOLN'S BODYGUARD IS MISSING

By Ronald G. Shafer
*This article was first published in The Washington Post on May 2, 2021*

At the end of the Civil War, President Abraham Lincoln had no illusions about the frequent threats to kill him.

On the afternoon of April 14, 1865 — five days after the South surrendered — he told one of his bodyguards, William Crook, "I have perfect confidence in those who are around me, in every one of your men … But if it is to be done, it is impossible to prevent it."

That night, the 56-year-old Lincoln went to see a play at Ford's Theatre under the watch of a new guard, a D.C. police officer named John Frederick Parker. Parker's dereliction of duty helped change U.S. history.

Ironically, on this same day, Lincoln signed legislation to create the Secret Service — not to protect the president, but to combat counterfeiting. He was guarded round-the-clock by one member of a four-man security unit.

The 35-year-old Parker was an odd choice for this prestigious assignment. He had a record of unreliability, including drinking and frequenting a "house of ill repute" while on duty, according to the Abraham Lincoln Presidential Library and Museum in Springfield, Ill.

Confederate sympathizers were everywhere in the capital. One of them was the famous 26-year-old actor John Wilkes Booth, who that day went to Ford's Theatre to pick up his mail. The news was that Lincoln and Gen. Ulysses S. Grant planned to attend that evening's Good Friday performance of the popular comedy "Our American Cousin."

Lincoln wasn't keen about going that night but didn't want to disappoint the public. Grant and his wife decided to visit their children in New Jersey. So Lincoln and his wife, Mary Todd Lincoln, invited Clara Harris and her fiance, Maj. Henry

Rathbone, to join them. Parker reported for duty three hours late and was sent ahead to Ford's Theatre.

The presidential carriage got off to a late start. The play had begun when Lincoln and his party entered the theater well after 8 p.m. They went to a special presidential box above the right side of the stage. The actors stopped, and the crowd stood and cheered as the orchestra played "Hail to the Chief."

Parker had been provided a chair outside the door to the box in a passageway. But he couldn't see the play and soon moved into the audience. At intermission, he went to the Star Saloon next door. Whether he returned to the theater is still a mystery.

Booth was in and out of the theater. At a little past 9 p.m., he took a saddled horse to the stage door at the back of the theater and left it there with a stage hand. Then he went to the saloon, where, according to the Washington Star, he tapped impatiently on the bar while calling for "Brandy, brandy, brandy."

Booth returned to the theater about 10 p.m. while the third act was underway. He made his way to the door to the passageway and went in. He wedged a piece of wood against the door so that it couldn't be opened from the outside. He moved up the narrow passageway carrying a one-shot Derringer in one hand and a dagger in the other.

Parker's chair was empty; there was no guard in front of the two doors to the presidential box. Lincoln was sitting in a cushioned rocking chair with his wife on his right. Booth waited for a line in the play that he knew would draw a loud laugh, helping to drown out the sound of a gunshot.

The lone actor on the stage said of a busybody Mrs. Mountchessington: "Don't know the manners of good society, eh? Well, I guess I know enough to turn you inside out, old gal — you sockdologizing old man-trap!"

With that, at 10:14 p.m., Booth burst into the box and shot Lincoln in the back of the head. The president slumped forward, the New York Times reported.

When Rathbone tried to grab the assassin, Booth slashed the major's arm with his knife, drawing blood. Booth leaped on the front railing, "raised his right hand, flourishing a dagger in theatrical style" and shouted "Sic semper tyrannis" (thus always to tyrants), an eye witness wrote in the Washington Star.

FIGURE 26: THE ASSASSINATION OF LINCOLN AT FORD'S THEATRE

As Booth jumped to the stage, one spur caught on a flag, and he landed awkwardly, injuring his right leg. He shouted "The South is revenged" as he ran for the stage door, bumping into the orchestra leader and cutting the musician's clothing with his dagger. Men rushed forward yelling, "Hang him. Hang him.

Many people in the audience at first thought the gunshot was part of the play. Then Mary Todd Lincoln screamed.

Poet Walt Whitman later wrote this account from New York:

"A moment's hush — a scream — the cry of murder — Mrs. Lincoln leaning out of the box, with ashy cheeks and lips, with involuntary cry, pointing to the retreating figure 'He has killed the president.' And still a moment's strange incredulous suspense — and then the deluge! then that mixture of horror, noises, uncertainty (the sound somewhere back, of a horse's clattering with speed) …

"And in the midst of all that pandemonium…the life blood from those veins the best and sweetest in the land, drops slowly down and death's ooze already begins its little bubbles on the lips."

A doctor quickly arrived, but Lincoln was barely alive. Amid Mrs. Lincoln's "heart rending shrieks," the president's long, limp form was carried across the street to the Petersen House, where he died at 7:22 the next morning.

At about the same time Lincoln was shot, two associates of Booth forced their way into the nearby Lafayette Square home of Secretary of State William Seward, and one of them began stabbing him about the head. Seward was saved when his bodyguard stopped the attacker.

A third man was supposed to kill Vice President Andrew Johnson in his room at the Kirkwood House hotel but lost his nerve. Booth had planned to use his knife to also kill Grant.

Booth was on the run. He had hoped the South would rise again.

War Secretary Edwin Stanton announced a $100,000 reward (equal to $1.7 million today) for Booth's capture. Federal soldiers tracked him to a tobacco barn in Port Royal, Va., on April 26. They set the barn on fire and shot Booth dead when he resisted. In June, a military court convicted eight Booth accomplices, and four were hanged.

Strangely, the disappearing Parker drew scant attention. He was next seen at six the following morning at the police station when he tried to book a prostitute. In May, a police board charged him with neglect of duty, but the charges were dismissed without any public explanation.

Parker returned to duty at the White House while Mary Todd Lincoln was still there. The widow angrily accused him of "helping to murder the president," according to a book by her African American dressmaker, Elizabeth Keckley.

Parker claimed he had returned to his seat in the audience, Keckley wrote. He said, "I did not see the assassin enter the box… I did not believe that anyone would try to kill so good a man in such a public place, and the belief made me careless."

If Parker had stayed at his post, "I believe President Lincoln might not have been murdered by Booth," Lincoln's other bodyguard Crook wrote in his memoir.

Parker never was penalized for having abandoned his post when the president was assassinated, but he was fired in 1868. His offense: sleeping while on duty.

# CHAPTER 26

# THE MOST PROLIFIC
# PRESIDENTIAL GOLFER

By Ronald G. Shafer
*This article was first published in The Washington Post on April 6, 2019*

As world events swirl around him, the president finds time to golf. Not even foreign threats of war can keep him from hitting the links.

That duffer in chief was Democratic President Woodrow Wilson. From 1913 to 1919, Wilson played nearly 1,200 rounds of golf — more than any U.S. president in history. Beating that record will be a challenge even for President Donald Trump, a serial golfer who a new book alleges is also a serial cheater.

Wilson golfed no matter what the weather. He golfed in snowstorms with golf balls that were painted red so his caddie could find them. "Secret Service men following him are not over enthusiastic about winter golf," United Press reported.

He golfed in summer rains. He wasn't deterred after burning his left hand by grabbing the hot exhaust pipe of the fighter tank Brittanica during a demonstration ride on the White House grounds. Within three weeks, Wilson had "developed into a professional one-handed player and can be seen on the links" almost every day, one newspaper said.

Wilson saw golf as a diversion from the long, high-pressure days of his job. "Each stroke requires your whole attention and seems the most important thing in life," he said.

Wilson usually played at local courses with the White House physician, Cary T. Grayson, who had recommended the exercise. They generally played nine holes during the week and 18 on weekends.

Golf even led Wilson to romance. In the spring of 1915, the president and Grayson rushed back to the White House in wet clothes and muddy shoes after their game was cut short by a rainstorm. Wilson turned a corner and ran into a visitor, the widow Edith Bolling Galt.

"We met face to face," she later recalled. "The two gentleman, I am sorry to say," weren't "well-attired. Their golf suits, as I found out later, were made by a cheap tailor the President had used for years." Despite Wilson's outfit, Galt and the president had an immediate attraction. Wilson's wife had died a year before. That December the 59-year-old president married 43-year-old Galt. Wilson began golfing with his new wife, who reportedly was the better player.

FIGURE 27: PRESIDENT WOODROW WILSON

Even with his frequent games, Wilson was a terrible golfer, partly because of a vision problem. When playing 18 holes, "seldom did his score rise above 100 because upon reaching three digits he was inclined to pack up his clubs and quit," Scott Berg wrote in his book "Wilson."

The president's "got a three-quarter swing. He would play better if his swing was a little fuller," Wilson's 11-year-old caddie at the Myopia Hunt Golf Club in Magnolia, Mass. said in a newspaper interview. Wilson also putts too fast, the kid caddie said, but "his direction on drives is quite good."

Hardly anything could keep Wilson away from the golf course. On April 2, 1917, he prepared an evening speech to a joint session of Congress seeking to declare war on Germany in World War I. But first he golfed with Mrs. Wilson that morning. At the Paris Peace Conference in early 1919, Wilson found time to sneak off to the links at Versailles.

Wilson continued his nearly daily golf until October of that year, when he suffered a massive stroke. He remained in office, but his golfing days were over.

Wilson wasn't the first president to golf. His predecessor, 300-plus-pound William Howard Taft, helped to popularize the game in America. Wilson's successor, Warren Harding, also often hit the links. Harding, dressed in knickers, told reporters at one news conference: "Take it easy on me, boys. I want to get out to play some golf."

The most prolific presidential golfer next to Wilson was Dwight D. Eisenhower, who played over 800 rounds. Ike even had a putting green installed at the White House. President Bill Clinton also was an active golfer.

In the 2016 presidential campaign, Barack Obama's golfing was targeted by Republican candidate Trump, who tweeted: "Can you believe that, with all the problems and difficulties facing the U.S., President Obama spent the day playing golf." Trump told a rally that, if elected, "I'm going to be working for you. I'm not going to have time to play golf."

In his first two years, Trump has visited his golf courses more than 150 times, according to the Associated Press. That compares with 306 golf outings by Obama in eight years. Trump is rated one of the best presidential golfers in history, but the honesty of his scores has been challenged in a new book, "Trump, Commander In Cheat: How Golf Explains Trump" by Rick Reilly. "To say 'Donald Trump' cheats' is like saying "Michael Phelps swims,' " Reilly asserted. "He cheats at the highest level." Trump has called Reilly a "very dishonest writer."

Nobody accused Wilson of cheating at golf. In early 1920, when Wilson began to take his first auto rides since his stroke had confined him to the White House, the Washington Examiner reported: "He expressed a yearning to again play golf, his favorite pastime."

# CHAPTER 27

# THE FIRST WHITE HOUSE CORRESPONDENT

By Ronald G. Shafer
*This article was first published in The Washington Post on April 29, 2023*

In 1896, an editor at the Washington Evening Star sought to test a cub reporter, 29-year-old William Wallace Price. So he sent Price somewhere reporting went to die: the White House.

At the time, Washington reporters focused on Congress and rarely had access to the White House. The Star editor, Harry Godwin, knew that then-President Grover Cleveland disliked the press, too.

But the 300-pound Price posted himself right outside the White House gate, day after day, rain or shine. And he ambushed those going through it.

"When politicians calling on President Cleveland emerged, 'Fatty' Price buttonholed them and milked them of what news they were willing to give down," New York Times reporter Delbert Clark wrote in his 1941 book "Washington Dateline."

Price, considered the country's first full-time White House reporter, went on to co-found the White House Correspondents' Association, whose 2023 dinner President Biden addressed Saturday. His methods helped transform the relationship between presidents and the press, an evolution Price captured in his own writings.

FIGURE 28: WILLIAM PRICE

Price, who launched a column called "At The White House" in 1897, got so many scoops staking out the gates that other newsmen soon began joining him. The growing number of what Price called "the newspaper gang of the White House" gained wider access that March, with the arrival of President William McKinley, who had seen the value of press coverage during his 1896 campaign from his Ohio front porch.

McKinley loved "going among the people" on railroad trips, Price later wrote. "One car and sometimes two cars would be set aside for the press."

Once, the president was invited to tour the "Biltmore" estate of George Vanderbilt, but not with reporters. "Then I will not accept the invitation," McKinley responded. He went, with the newsmen.

White House officials generally talked to all reporters anonymously, a reality Price understood. "It is the business of the reporter to know how to handle the information given him so as to get the news into his paper and at the same time conceal the source of the material," he wrote in 1914. "To blunder in handling information of this kind, making trouble for his informant and others, would be unpardonable."

When the Spanish-American War began, in 1898, McKinley invited reporters inside the White House to use a press table on the second floor. But there wasn't a separate press room until Theodore Roosevelt, who assumed office after McKinley was assassinated, expanded the White House in 1902, creating the West Wing. It was a small room, with three telephones, just off the lobby.

Roosevelt used his press access to put his spin on the news. "His face lathered and wearing one of his famous grins," he talked "gayly to his press friends" while he was being shaved, Price wrote.

Roosevelt "put into useful practice the view that to get to the public first with your own opinions and facts was equivalent to hitting the other fellow the first blow in a personal encounter," Price said. He "left many a political corpse in the arena by beating the other fellow to the newspaper and getting his side fixed in the public mind."

William Howard Taft didn't share Roosevelt's enthusiasm for the press, but he established a personal relationship with Price, who called Taft "boss" while Taft called him "Bill." Price, who also wore about the same suit size as the 330-pound 27th president, wrote that Taft planned to stay out of politics after he lost the 1912 election. "I suppose Bill Price thinks that because he is wearing my pants, he is absorbing some of my thoughts," Taft complained, in a note to another reporter.

Press relations got off to a fast start under Taft's successor, Woodrow Wilson. Wilson, a Democrat, initially met regularly with reporters and held the first formal presidential news conference on March 15, 1913, with about 100 reporters in the Oval Office. His remarks were off the record.

Price the next year helped create the White House Correspondents' Association, and he was elected its first chairman. The WHCA issued a photo of 28 newsmen surrounding a smiling Wilson. At one press briefing, Price, "big, fat, florid and overpowering, drew a laugh from the President by an audacious remark," New York Times columnist Arthur Krock wrote in 1914. But relations soured when Wilson complained that some reporters were publishing his off-the-record comments, and he curtailed the gatherings.

Price, meanwhile, curtailed his beat reporting in 1917, leaving the Star to be chief editorial writer at the Washington Times. He stayed on, though, as the WHCA's leader — and set the jovial tone for its dinners as toastmaster.

President Warren G. Harding, an Ohio newspaper publisher, resumed press briefings after his election, and the WHCA celebrated in 1921 by holding its first banquet, at Washington's Arlington Hotel, with 50 newsmen in attendance. Calvin Coolidge in 1924 became the first president to attend, giving a serious speech about tax cuts. But, the next year, "Silent Cal" uncharacteristically delivered a witty, off-the-record talk that had his press audience "in an uproar," the Star reported.

It was a harbinger of things to come. The dinner took off as a social event during World War II, featuring variety shows by Hollywood stars such as Frank Sinatra and Bob Hope. Danny Kaye and Jimmy Durante sang and performed comedy routines before 900 people at President Franklin D. Roosevelt's last correspondents' dinner, in March 1945. President John F. Kennedy, who refused to attend the 1962 dinner until women were allowed, began its custom of presidents making on-the-record humorous remarks. The Democrat joked that after conferring with voters while vacationing in wealthy Palm Beach, Fla., "I came back to Washington, and I am against my entire program."

Every president since Coolidge has attended the dinner at least once except for Donald Trump, but such an atmosphere hasn't suited every president as well. Richard M. Nixon complained in a 1971 memo that, at his first news conference after that year's dinner, "where I played the 'good sport role,' the reporters were considerably more bad-mannered and vicious than usual."

Nixon couldn't, at least, say he was ambushed.

# CHAPTER 28

# PRESIDENTIAL TV PRESS CONFERENCES

By Ronald G. Shafer
*This article was first published in The Washington Post on November 18, 2018*

"What have you done for women?" one persistent reporter pressed then-President John F. Kennedy.

"Well, I'm sure we haven't done enough," Kennedy responded with a laugh to Gannett's May Craig in November 1961.

The exchange was much more friendly than the recent confrontation between President Trump and CNN's Jim Acosta that prompted the administration to ban the reporter from the White House. CNN dropped its lawsuit against the White House after officials told the network that they would restore Acosta's press credentials as long as he followed a new set of rules.

Acosta isn't the first White House reporter to make waves at presidential news conferences. Craig, wearing a hat with flowers, was one of the first attention-getting reporters. Sarah McClendon and Helen Thomas posed tough questions for decades. ABC's Sam Donaldson also drew notice with his aggressive questioning of presidents. But none were banned from the White House.

Reporter banishment is a new chapter in presidential news conferences, which began with Woodrow Wilson in 1913. President Eisenhower started the first televised news conferences in 1955, but these were recorded and selected clips were released to the press later.

Kennedy began live televised news conferences on Jan. 25, 1961. He often called on 72-year-old Craig, who was a seasoned war correspondent. On the woman question, Kennedy answered further: "I must say I am a strong believer in equal pay for equal work, and I think that we ought to do better than we're doing. And I'm glad that you reminded me of it, Mrs. Craig."

McClendon, who headed a group of small newspapers in Texas, brought what she called "a pushy and sometimes confrontational" style to news conferences. In 1958, she pressed Eisenhower on why his administration wasn't doing more to combat the recession. The president's face reddened, and he clenched his fist as he began his answer: "Now, look.."

McClendon's tactics sometimes got results. At a news conference in early 1974 she complained to then-President Richard Nixon that some Vietnam veterans were running into delays getting government checks to pay for college. When Nixon said the problem had been addressed, McClendon retorted: "No, you're just misinformed."

The president later said in a radio broadcast that because of questions from "a very spirited reporter" he had ordered changes. "Sarah McClendon," Nixon once said, "asks questions that no man would ever think of."

Not everybody appreciated the "little lady with the big voice," as McClendon described herself. President George H.W. Bush warned her, "The loudest voice won't always get recognized because it isn't fair to the others." Eric Sevareid of CBS News said McClendon was a "lady who has been known to give rudeness a bad name at times." McClendon died in 2003 at age 92.

Helen Thomas started covering the Kennedy White House for United Press International in 1961. She immediately gained a reputation as a tough questioner. Kennedy said of her, "Helen would be a nice girl if she'd ever get rid of that pad and pencil."

FIGURE 29: PRESIDENT GERALD FORD AND HELEN THOMAS

Thomas didn't stop asking pesky questions. When President Clinton called on Thomas to ask the first question following revelations about his sexual relationship with Monica Lewinsky, Thomas said, "You may not like it." She then pressed Clinton about his previous denials of any involvement. When George H.W. Bush announced that the defense budget wouldn't be cut after the collapse of the Soviet Union and the fall of the Berlin Wall, Thomas asked him, "Who's the enemy?" In 2006, she asked President George W. Bush, "Why did you really go to war" in Iraq?

In 1975, Thomas became the first female president of the White House Correspondents' Association. She quit UPI in 2000 and soon joined the Hearst newspapers. Her long career abruptly ended under a cloud of controversy in 2010 after Thomas, who was of Lebanese descent, said Jews should leave Palestinian territories. She died in 2013 at age 92.

ABC's Donaldson became known for shouting questions at presidents Jimmy Carter and Ronald Reagan. Donaldson was all business all the time. When Reagan talked to reporters about his meeting with Mother Teresa, Donaldson bellowed: "What about the tax bill?"

Some confrontations took place in the press briefing room that Nixon had installed over the White House swimming pool. Reagan's press secretary James Brady joked the president planned to install a button on his podium that he could press to open a trap door under reporters "who got out of line." The briefing room is now named after Brady, who was shot and badly wounded during the 1981 attempted assassination of Reagan. Brady died in 2014.

Donaldson's bluster never led to his being banned. Indeed, Reagan seemed to enjoy the confrontations. Once when the TV newsman asked Reagan whether he took any blame for the lingering recession in the early 1980s, the president quipped, "Yes, because for many years I was a Democrat."

Donaldson, who retired in 2013, is supporting the CNN lawsuit challenging the White House ouster of Acosta after Trump called the reporter "a rude, terrible person." Donaldson, now 84, said, "President Harry Truman summed up the necessary interplay between a president and the press corps when he advised government officials at every level: 'If you can't take the heat, get out of the kitchen.'"

As for White House reporters pushing for answers, Helen Thomas once said, in the arena of presidential news conferences, "There are no rude questions."

# CHAPTER 29

# SPOOFING THE PRESIDENTS

By Ronald G. Shafer
*This article was first published in The Washington Post on March 19, 2019*

The president of the United States was furious at being lampooned in yet another TV comedy skit. So he phoned the head of the TV network at 3 a.m. to complain.

The perturbed POTUS wasn't Donald Trump, who recently tweeted that federal regulators should look into the "not funny" attacks on him on "Saturday Night Live." The phone-calling president was Lyndon B. Johnson, who in 1967, long before Twitter, dialed up the head of CBS to gripe about "The Smothers Brothers Comedy Hour."

The weekly show hosted by folk-singing brothers Tom and Dick Smothers regularly skewered Johnson and his Vietnam War policies. The brothers sang the "Draft Dodger Rag" by Phil Ochs with such lines as, "I got eyes like a bat, and my feet are flat, and my asthma's getting worse."

When the United States imposed a travel ban to foreign countries, Tom Smothers looked in the camera and said, "Okay, all you guys in Vietnam, come on home." On the show, LBJ impersonator David Frye even joked about the president's "semi-beautiful daughters."

Johnson's two young daughters, Lynda and Luci, were fans of the highly watched show. But even they reportedly were upset about a mild skit on the top secret ingredients of LBJ's barbecue sauce. Johnson apparently was bugged to learn on the show that "the Russians were 20 years ahead of us in barbecue sauce," said one of the show's writers, Saul Illam.

For LBJ, it was the last straw. In the middle of the night, he phoned CBS head William Paley about the Smothers brothers, demanding that the TV executive "get those b------- off my back." That day, Paley asked the heads of CBS entertainment shows to get the brothers to back off, according to author David Bianculli in the book "Dangerously Funny: The Uncensored Story of the Smothers Brothers Comedy Hour."

Instead of backing off, the brothers Smothers doubled down. They booked antiwar folk singer Pete Seeger to perform a song called "Waist Deep in the Big Muddy" about a soldier being stuck in the mud. The lyrics were clearly aimed at Johnson and his Vietnam War policies. One part went: "We're waist deep in the mud. And the big fool says to push on."

At the last minute, CBS cut the song from the pre-taped show. The Smothers brothers cried foul and the next year succeeded in getting Seeger back on the show to sing the song uncut.

The brothers continued to push the political comedy envelop. In the fall of 1968, they featured Harry Belafonte singing "Don't Stop the Carnival" against a backdrop of news footage showing Chicago police pummeling antiwar protesters at the Democratic National Convention. CBS cut that segment, too. It was replaced by, of all things, an ad for Republican presidential candidate Richard M. Nixon.

"We were furious," Tom Smothers said later.

By then, Johnson had made a surprise announcement that he wouldn't seek reelection in 1968. The announcement prompted Tom and Dick Smothers to write LBJ a letter conceding they had "occasionally overstepped our bounds" in mocking him. Johnson responded with a letter praising the Smothers brothers' humor.

FIGURE 30: THE SMOTHERS BROTHERS

The Smothers brothers show continued its antiwar satire after Nixon's election. The new president wasn't amused. It was later revealed that some Nixon campaign funds were used to pay for a private investigation of the Smothers brothers.

Tensions continued between the brothers and CBS censors. Then in April of 1969 — just three months after Nixon had taken office — the network canceled the show. Its excuse was that Tom Smothers had failed to deliver an advance tape of a sensitive segment in a timely fashion. Smothers later claimed the network had killed off the show under pressure from the Nixon administration.

The brothers got the last laugh, sort of. They sued CBS for breach of contract. In 1973, a jury found in their favor and ordered CBS to pay the comedy duo more than $776,000. But this was far less than the brothers had sought.

The Smothers brothers weren't the first humorists to be targeted by a White House. In 1957, President Dwight D. Eisenhower's press secretary, James Hagerty, complained to the New York Herald Tribune about an account of his news conference in Paris by the paper's young Paris columnist, Art Buchwald. The satirical story, Hagerty complained, was "unadulterated rot." Buchwald responded: "Hagerty is wrong. I write adulterated rot."

Mort Sahl was a top stand-up comedian in 1960 when he got a phone call from Joseph Kennedy, the father of Sen. John F. Kennedy of Massachusetts, who was seeking the Democratic nomination for president. The elder Kennedy asked Sahl if he would "write some things for Johnny?" Sahl did. One of his jokes became the basis for a famous JFK quip about a telegram from his wealthy father. "Don't buy a single more vote than is necessary. I'll be d---ed if I'm going to pay for a landslide."

After Kennedy was elected, Sahl angered the Kennedy clan by poking fun at the new president. Sahl claimed that Joseph Kennedy, a onetime Hollywood mogul, blacklisted him in clubs across the country, causing his income to plummet.

When Nixon campaigned in 1968, he tried to show he had a sense of humor by appearing on the popular TV comedy show "Rowan and Martin's Laugh-In." The show's tag line was "Sock it to me." In his cameo appearance, Nixon looked into the camera and said, "Sock it to me?"

But like Trump, Nixon hated the press and comics who made fun of him. His "enemies list" included two comedians, Bill Cosby and Dick Gregory, both African Americans.

Trump regularly rails at the barbs of late night comedians. He tweeted Sunday about a rerun of an SNL skit: "It's truly incredible that shows like Saturday Night Live, not funny/no talent, can spend all their time knocking the same person (me), over & over, without so much of a mention of 'the other side.' ... Should Federal Election Commission and/or FCC look into this?"

On Twitter, there was amazement that the president had gone after a rerun. And SNL star Leslie Jones fired back on Instagram, posting a photo of Trump's tweet and her own reaction: "This guy is an idiot. It was a rerun you moron!!"

The Trump tweets are in sharp contrast to that letter Lyndon Johnson sent to the Smothers brothers in 1968. It read: "It is part of the price of leadership of this great and free nation to be the target of clever satirists. You have given the gift of laughter to our people. May we never grow so somber or self-important that we fail to appreciate the humor in our lives."

# CHAPTER 30

# PRESIDENTIAL PORTRAITS

By Ronald G. Shafer
*This article was first published in The Washington Post on September 7, 2022*

President Theodore Roosevelt griped that his made him look like "a mewing cat." President Lyndon B. Johnson called his "the ugliest thing I ever saw." President Ronald Reagan ordered a do-over.

All of the presidents were complaining about their official White House portraits, which are a long-standing tradition. Or they were until President Donald Trump ended the practice of sitting presidents unveiling the official portraits of their predecessors — nearly uninterrupted for four decades — by not holding a ceremony for former president Barack Obama.

Trump has never explained why he skipped the portrait ritual. But on Wednesday, President Joe Biden, who served as Obama's vice president, will resume the tradition by unveiling the official portraits of the nation's first Black president and former first lady Michelle Obama at the White House.

The unveiling ceremonies, which began in 1978, are traditionally "bipartisan events with warm greetings and collegial speeches exchanged by the president and their predecessor," according to the White House Historical Association. The non-profit group has been funding the official portraits of presidents and first ladies that hang in the White House since 1965.

The presidential portraits in the White House date back to Gilbert Stuart's iconic painting of George Washington. First lady Dolley Madison famously saved the painting when she and President James Madison fled the president's mansion as the British torched the place in 1814

"Presidents and first ladies typically select their respective artists before leaving the White House," the association said. But sometimes they aren't happy with the initial results.

In 1902, Roosevelt detested his portrait by French artist Theobald Chartran so much that he hid it in a closet and then had it destroyed. He complained that it made him look more like a meek kitty than "the powerful president." He chose artist John Singer Sargent to paint a new one that made him look more macho.

Johnson refused to accept his portrait by noted artist Peter Hurd, who showed him standing in front of the Capitol and holding a book. In the portrait, "Johnson looms like some hulking cow hand," wrote Time magazine columnist Hugh Sidey. "The mouth that Hurd has painted is firm, even capable of meanness," and the Vietnam War and Watts riots are reflected "in the furrows of the brow and eyes."

Johnson switched to Elizabeth Shoumatoff, who had painted the official portrait of President Franklin D. Roosevelt. In her portrait, also with the Capitol in the background, Johnson looks "unbelievably pleasant," Sidey wrote. But between the two paintings, he wrote, those who knew Johnson "will recall with fondness 'the other one' — the real one."

President Richard M. Nixon didn't have time to sit for a portrait before he resigned in 1974 because of the Watergate scandal. He finally had one done by Alexander Clayton, showing the former president sitting at his Oval Office desk. The painting turned up on a White House wall in 1981, "placed without fanfare," news services reported.

FIGURE 31: PETER HURD'S JOHNSON PORTRAIT

But Nixon wasn't satisfied with the painting. In 1984, he donated a new portrait by James Anthony Wills, who had painted President Dwight D. Eisenhower's portrait. "He liked it better," said a federal official.

The official unveilings of presidential and first lady portraits began in May 1978, when Democratic President Jimmy Carter hosted former Republican president Gerald Ford and Betty Ford. The former president said he saw the final portraits by Everett Raymond Kinstler only moments before the ceremony began. "In my case, considering what Kinstler had to work with, he did well," he said.

Carter, who had defeated Ford in the 1976 election after Watergate, praised Ford as "a man who led our country in time of crisis and strain and who bought capability and knowledge to heal our wounds. No one appreciates him more than I do."

Much of the focus was on Mrs. Ford, who had just left four weeks of alcohol and drug rehabilitation. As a crusader for the treatment of drug and alcohol abuse, she "has earned the admiration of our nation for her courage and complete candor," Carter said.

At Carter's request, there was no public unveiling of the White House portraits of him and his wife, Rosalynn. But Reagan agreed to resume the tradition after he left office in 1989.

Reagan's portrait unveiling was delayed because he and his wife, Nancy, didn't care for the first effort by Aaron Shikler, who had painted the official portraits of President John F. Kennedy and Jacqueline Kennedy. Nancy Reagan liked Shikler's painting of her in a red dress, but she thought her husband's portrait lacked that "twinkle in his eye."

Shikler had to start over. The final version was unveiled in November 1989 by President George H.W. Bush, who had been Reagan's vice president. "When the announcer here said 'Mr. President,' why I fell back to where I comfortably was for eight years," Bush quipped. But the Shikler portrait was only a placeholder. In 1991, it was replaced with a new Reagan portrait by Kinstler.

Bush was pleased with his portrait by Herbert Abrams when President Bill Clinton unveiled it in 1995. "I'm inclined to think it's pretty darn good," Bush declared. Clinton told the former president, "If I look half as good as you do when I leave office, I'll be a happy man."

But Barbara Bush wasn't thrilled with Abrams's matronly portrait of her. So 10 years later, she had a second painting done by Charles Fagan that showed the former first lady with a photo of her pet spaniel, Millie.

In June 2004, President George W. Bush welcomed Bill and Hillary Clinton when unveiling their portraits. Bush praised Bill Clinton for "the forward-looking spirit that Americans like in a president." Clinton responded, "I hope that I live long enough to see American politics return to vigorous debates where we argue who's right and wrong, and not who's good and bad." The paintings of both Clintons were done by artist Simmie Knox.

The Obamas unveiled the portraits of Bush and first lady Laura Bush by John Howard Sanden in May 2012. Obama lauded Bush's "strength and resolve" after the terrorist attacks of Sept. 11, 2001. He also thanked him for leaving behind a "really good TV sports package" at the White House.

We are overwhelmed," Bush responded. The former president fought back tears as he thanked his father, whose portrait already hung in the White House.

"We may have our differences politically," Obama said, "but the presidency transcends those differences."

# SECTION 8

# VICE PRESIDENTS

# CHAPTER 31

# A BURR UNDER THE SADDLE

By Ronald G. Shafer
*This article was first published in The Washington Post on September 26, 2022*

On Aug. 3, 1807, in Richmond, Va., Chief Justice John Marshall opened the trial of former vice president Aaron Burr. The charge: treason against the United States. Burr was accused of plotting an armed insurrection against the government.

More than two centuries later, potential treason is being discussed again following the latest twists in the Justice Department's investigation of former president Donald Trump, including the revelation that the FBI discovered a top secret document about a foreign nation's nuclear capabilities at Trump's estate in Florida. Former federal prosecutor Glenn Kirschner recently said on MSNBC that Trump's role in igniting "an armed attack on the Capitol … may actually amount to treason." So far the Justice Department hasn't indicated what charges, if any, might result from its probe, though Trump is facing at least eight criminal and civil proceedings.

Only about 30 people have ever been charged with treason in the United States, and Burr was the highest-ranking official to go on trial. By 1807, he was an outcast from both political parties. He had turned off many Democratic-Republicans when, as Thomas Jefferson's presumed running mate in 1800, Burr had tried to claim the presidency after both men received the same number of electoral votes. Then, as vice president in 1804, Burr shot and killed Federalist Alexander Hamilton in a duel. Burr also presided over the controversial 1805 impeachment trial of Supreme Court Justice Samuel Chase

After Jefferson won reelection in 1804 with a new vice president, George Clinton, Burr took several trips to the U.S. Southwest and launched the "Burr Conspiracy." He assembled an armed force, allegedly to capture a part of Mexico (now Texas) from Spain and to take control of New Orleans in the U.S. Louisiana

Territory, and then to persuade western states to join an independent nation he would head.

In December 1806, Jefferson warned that "sundry persons" were conspiring to form an illegal military expedition. In January, he named Burr as "a prime mover" of the treasonous conspiracy and said Burr's guilt was "placed beyond question." Meanwhile, he pressed Congress to pass what became the Insurrection Act of 1807, which gave the president the authority to send in troops to quell uprisings.

In February 1807, Burr was arrested in Alabama and taken by military guard on horseback about 900 miles to Richmond, then a town of about 6,000 people, of whom more than 2,000 were enslaved. Burr was put under guard at the city's Eagle Tavern hotel. Public testimony before a grand jury began on May 22 in Richmond's federal circuit court.

Crowds of people swarmed into Richmond. "They were so numerous that the trial had to be held in the legislative chamber of the State House, which was fitted with sandboxes to catch the flying tobacco juice," wrote R. Kent Newmyer, author of "The Treason Trial of Aaron Burr." Newspapers reported that one street orator was future president Andrew Jackson, who berated Jefferson for "persecuting his innocent friend."

Others called for Burr to find justice at the end of a rope. "May his treachery to his country exalt him to the scaffold, and hemp be his escort to the Republic of dust and ashes," a Baltimore man wrote.

At the time, the Supreme Court's six justices sometimes presided over circuit courts. Chief Justice Marshall, who lived in Richmond, took the lead on the Burr case, which featured a dazzling array of legal talent. Leading the prosecution were George Hay, a son-in-law of future president James Monroe, and William Wirt, a future U.S. attorney general. Defense lawyers included former secretary of state Edmund Randolph, former attorney general Charles Lee and Luther Martin, a delegate to the Constitutional Convention.

But the defense's primary leader "was Burr himself," wrote Joseph P. Brady in his 1913 book "The Trial of Aaron Burr." "He was keenly alive to every proceeding" and "no move was made, or point conceded, without his sanction." Jefferson provided guidance to the prosecution. At Burr's request, Marshall took the unprecedented step of issuing a subpoena to the president to provide certain documents and even to appear in court. Jefferson, citing the Constitution's separation of powers, never complied.

FIGURE 32: AARON BURR

The government's key witness was army commander Gen. James Wilkinson, the Louisiana Territory's first governor, who had joined in Burr's early plans before turning on him. Wilkinson, dressed in his military uniform, "strutted into court . . . swelling like a turkey-cock," novelist Washington Irving wrote in a newspaper. Wilkinson's testimony led to Burr's indictment for treason. Burr, who had been free on bail, was put in the nearby federal penitentiary.

The treason trial began at noon on Aug. 3. Prosecutor Hay presented a broad interpretation of treason to the 12-man jury, expanding on the indictment's charge that Burr had begun forming a military force on Blennerhassett Island in the Ohio River near Marietta, Ohio. On Dec. 10, 1806, the indictment alleged, up to 30 people were assembled, "armed and arrayed in a warlike manner" with "guns, swords [and] other warlike weapons," being there "unlawfully, maliciously and traitorously" and preparing to make war against the United States, starting with an attack on New Orleans. Hay conceded Burr himself was in Kentucky that day.

The treason clause of the U.S. Constitution sets a high bar. It reads in part: "Treason against the United States shall consist only in levying war against them, or in adhering to their enemies, giving them aid and comfort. No person shall be convicted of treason unless on the testimony of two witnesses to the same overt act, or on confession in open court."

Marshall, who had been appointed to the Supreme Court in 1801 by lame-duck Federalist President John Adams, leading Jefferson to accuse the Federalists of stealing the seat, adopted a strict interpretation of the clause. In his three-hour summation and instructions to the jury, he sided with defense arguments. He said an "overt" act of war must be "proved by two witnesses. It is not proved by a single witness." He added, "No man can be convicted of treason who was not present when the war was levied."

Marshall left the jury little choice. After 25 minutes, the jurors returned with a verdict: not guilty. Jefferson was furious. "It now appears we have no law but the will of the judge," he fumed. Effigies of Marshall and Burr were hung in several cities. Burr was soon a free man.

Historians still debate just how serious the Burr insurrection was, but he was widely considered a traitor at the time. He moved to England for five years, then returned to New York. In 1833, he married a wealthy widow who was 19 years his junior and who soon saw her husband losing her money in costly land speculation.

Burr died at age 80 on Sept. 14, 1836 — the same day his divorce was finalized. His former wife's divorce lawyer was Alexander Hamilton Jr.

# CHAPTER 32

# THE JOHN TYLER RULE OF DEAD PRESIDENTS

By Ronald G. Shafer
*This article was first published in The Washington Post on March 31, 2019*

On April 5, 1841, two men on horseback galloped up at sunrise to Vice President John Tyler's home in Williamsburg, Va. They were there to deliver startling news: President William Henry Harrison had died of pneumonia after only a month in office. Tyler rushed to Washington, arriving at 4 a.m. the next day. At noon, Tyler was sworn in as Harrison's successor at Brown's Indian Queen Hotel.

But was Tyler really the president? The 68-year-old Harrison, a military hero nicknamed "Old Tippecanoe" after one of his battles against the Indians, was the first commander in chief to die in office in U.S. history. Nobody was sure how succession was supposed to work. The Constitution stated that "in case of the removal of the President from office, or of his death, resignation, or inability to discharge the powers and duties of the said office, the same shall devolve on the Vice President." But it didn't say the vice president would become president.

Many people believed Tyler was only the "acting president." One congressman proposed calling him "the Vice-President, on whom, by the death of the late President, the powers and duties of the office of President have devolved." The public gave Tyler another name: "His Accidency."

The only reason the Whig Party had picked the former Virginia senator as Harrison's running mate in the 1840 election was to woo Southern voters. They ran on a ticket known as "Tippecanoe and Tyler Too" — a slogan so catchy that it is still remembered 170 years later. Harrison lived in Ohio, though he grew up a few miles down the road from Tyler in Charles City County, Va., near Williamsburg.

Nobody expected that Tyler, a 51-year-old slave owner, would ever become president, according to former president John Quincy Adams. Tyler, Adams said, was a man "with talents not above mediocrity, and a spirit incapable of expansion to the dimensions of the station on which he has been cast by the hand of Providence."

Tyler, courtly but strong-minded, insisted he was president without reservation.

At his first Cabinet meeting, Secretary of State Daniel Webster told Tyler that Harrison and Cabinet members had voted on decisions, and Harrison went with the majority.

"I beg your pardon," Tyler politely responded. "I am the president, and I shall be responsible for my administration."

That June, after vigorous debate, Congress confirmed that Tyler was president with the title and powers of the office. And his ascension to the Oval Office created what was known as the "Tyler Precedent," which would continue as the de facto law of the land for the next 125 years.

President Tyler soon ran into big problems with the Whig-controlled Congress. As one observer noted, "There was more rhyme than reason" to the famous campaign slogan "Tippecanoe and Tyler Too." Tyler had only recently switched to the Whig Party but didn't share many of its views. He vetoed so many bills that the Whigs kicked him out of their party, and his entire Cabinet resigned except for Webster.

FIGURE 33: JOHN TYLER

Whigs protested outside the White House and hanged Tyler in effigy. One Virginia congressman proposed impeaching the "acting" president. The move failed, thus avoiding another succession crisis since Tyler never had a vice president.

Tyler briefly campaigned for another term as an independent in 1844 but dropped out. He left office in early 1845 after Democrat James K. Polk was elected. Tyler's main accomplishment was paving the way for the Republic of Texas to be annexed as a slave state in 1845. The town of Tyler, Tex., was named in his honor.

Tyler and his young wife, Julia, moved their family to a slave plantation in Charles City County. Since the Whigs considered him to be an outlaw like Robin Hood, Tyler named the plantation Sherwood Forest.

When the Civil War broke out, Tyler sided with the South. He was a member of the Confederate House of Representatives when he died at a Richmond hotel in 1862 at age 71. The New York Times obituary described Tyler as "the most unpopular public man that had ever held any office in the United States."

But the "Tyler Precedent" lived on. When President Zachary Taylor died of food poisoning in 1850, Vice President Millard Fillmore became president without controversy. The precedent was invoked six more times for presidents Andrew Johnson, Chester Arthur, Theodore Roosevelt, Calvin Coolidge, Harry Truman and Lyndon Johnson.

After President John F. Kennedy was assassinated in 1963, Democratic Sen. Birch Bayh of Indiana led an effort to amend the Constitution to clarify succession as well as how a president can be removed from office. Congress passed the 25th Amendment in 1965. After ratification by the states, the amendment came into play in 1974 when Richard Nixon resigned and Vice President Gerald Ford became president.

The 25th Amendment codified the precedent for presidential succession that began in 1841. All because John Tyler insisted that he wouldn't be called anything else but "Mr. President."

# CHAPTER 33

# THE VICE PRESIDENT'S ENSLAVED WIFE

By Ronald G. Shafer
*This article was first published in The Washington Post on February 7, 2021*

She was born enslaved and remained that way her entire life, even after she became Richard Mentor Johnson's "bride."

Johnson, a Kentucky congressman who eventually became the nation's ninth vice president in 1837, couldn't legally marry Julia Chinn. Instead the couple exchanged vows at a local church with a wedding celebration organized by the enslaved people at his family's plantation in Great Crossing, according to Miriam Biskin, who wrote about Chinn decades ago.

Chinn died nearly four years before Johnson took office. But because of controversy over her, Johnson is the only vice president in American history who failed to receive enough electoral votes to be elected. The Senate voted him into office.

The couple's story is complicated and fraught, historians say. As an enslaved woman, Chinn could not consent to a relationship, and there's no record of how she regarded him. Though she wrote to Johnson during his lengthy absences from Kentucky, the letters didn't survive.

Amrita Chakrabarti Myers, who is working on a book about Chinn, wrote about the hurdles in a blog post for the Association of Black Women Historians. "While doing my research, I was struck by how Julia had been erased from the history books," wrote Myers, a history professor at Indiana University. "Nobody knew who she was. The truth is that Julia (and Richard) are both victims of legacies of enslavement, interracial sex, and silence around black women's histories."

Johnson's life is far better documented.

FIGURE 34: VICE PRESIDENT RICHARD MENTOR JOHNSON

He was elected as a Democrat to the state legislature in 1802 and to Congress in 1806. The folksy, handsome Kentuckian gained a reputation as a champion of the common man. Back home in Great Crossing, he fathered a child with a local seamstress, but didn't marry her when his parents objected, according to the biography "The Life and Times of Colonel Richard M. Johnson of Kentucky." Then, in about 1811, Johnson, 31, turned to Chinn, 21, who had been enslaved at Blue Spring Plantation since childhood.

Johnson called Chinn "my bride." His "great pleasure was to sit by the fireplace and listen to Julia as she played on the pianoforte," Biskin wrote in her account.

The couple soon had two daughters, Imogene and Adaline. Johnson gave his daughters his last name and openly raised them as his children.

Johnson became a national hero during the War of 1812. At the Battle of the Thames in Canada, he led a horseback attack on the British and their Native American allies. He was shot five times but kept fighting. During the battle, the Shawnee chief Tecumseh was killed.

In 1819, "Colonel Dick" was elected to the U.S. Senate. When he was away in Washington for long periods, he left Chinn in charge of the 2,000-acre plantation and told his White employees that they should "act with the same propriety as if I were home."

Chinn's status was unique.

While enslaved women wore simple cotton dresses, Chinn's wardrobe "included fancy dresses that turned heads when Richard hosted parties," Christina Snyder wrote in her book "Great Crossings: Indians, Settlers & Slaves in the Age of Jackson." In 1825, Chinn and Johnson hosted the Marquis de Lafayette during his return to America.

FIGURE 35: JULIA CHINN

In the mid-1820s, Johnson opened on his plantation the Choctaw Academy, a federally funded boarding school for Native Americans. He hired a local Baptist minister as director. Chinn ran the academy's medical ward.

"Julia is as good as one half the physicians, where the complaint is not dangerous," Johnson wrote in a letter. He paid the academy's director extra to educate their daughters "for a future as free women."

Johnson tried to advance his daughters in local society, and both would later marry White men. But when he spoke at a local July Fourth celebration, the Lexington Observer reported, prominent White citizens wouldn't let Adaline sit with them in the pavilion. Johnson sent his daughter to his carriage, rushed through his speech and then angrily drove away.

When Johnson's father died, he willed ownership of Chinn to his son. He never freed his common-law wife.

"Whatever power Chinn had was dependent on the will and the whims of a White man who legally owned her," Snyder wrote.

Then, in 1833, Chinn died of cholera. It's unclear where she is buried. Johnson went on to even greater national prominence.

In 1836, President Andrew Jackson backed Vice President Martin Van Buren as his successor. At Jackson's urging, Van Buren — a fancy dresser who had never fought in war — picked war hero Johnson as his running mate. Nobody knew how the Shawnees' chief was slain in the War of 1812, but Johnson's campaign slogan was, "Rumpsey, Dumpsey. Johnson Killed Tecumseh."

Johnson's relationship with Chinn became a campaign issue. Southern newspapers denounced him as "the great Amalgamationist." A mocking cartoon showed a distraught Johnson with a hand over his face bewailing "the scurrilous attacks on the Mother of my Children."

Van Buren won the election, but Johnson's 147 electoral votes were one short of what he needed to be elected. Virginia's electors refused to vote for him. It was the only time Congress chose a vice president.

When Van Buren ran for reelection in 1840, Democrats declined to nominate Johnson at their Baltimore convention. It is the only time a party didn't pick any vice-presidential candidate. The spelling-challenged Jackson warned that Johnson would be a "dead wait" on the ticket.

"Old Dick" still ended up being the leading choice and campaigned around the country wearing his trademark red vest. But Van Buren lost to Johnson's former commanding officer, Gen. William Henry Harrison.

Johnson never remarried, but he reportedly had sexual relationships with other enslaved women who couldn't consent to the m. The former vice president won a final election to the Kentucky legislature in 1850, but died a short time later at the age of 70.

His brothers laid claim to his estate at the expense of his surviving daughter, Imogene, who was married to a White man named Daniel Pence.

"At some point in the early twentieth century," Myers wrote, "perhaps because of heightened fears of racism during the Jim Crow era, members of Imogene Johnson Pence's line, already living as white people, chose to stop telling their children that they were descended from Richard Mentor Johnson … and his black wife. It wasn't until the late 20th century that younger Pences, by then already in their 40s, 50s, and 60s, began discovering the truth of their heritage."

(Myers's book "The Vice President's Black Wife: The Untold Life of Julia Chinn" was published in 2023.)

# SECTION 9

# FINAL DAYS

# CHAPTER 34

# MEET MISS LILLIAN

By Ronald G. Shafer
*This article was first published in The Washington Post on February 26, 2023*

Former president Jimmy Carter, who recently entered home hospice care at age 98, called his mother "the most influential woman in my life." Lillian Carter, who famously joined the Peace Corps at 68, taught him, he said, "to take on new challenges and do what is right even though sometimes the consequences politically speaking were not good."

Many Americans remember "Miss Lillian," as she was widely known, as the most outspoken First Mother in history. When her son campaigned for president in 1976 by promising never to lie, "I told him to quit that stuff about he never lies and being Christian," she told Newsweek. "There are some things you don't have to go around saying."

Did she ever lie? "Oh, yes, I couldn't live without it," she told Redbook magazine.

"All I'm going to say about abortion — because it's pro and con — is that I think a woman's body should be hers," she told the Women's News Service, after her son said in 1976 that he believed abortions were "wrong," though he supported *Roe v. Wade.* "I believe in women having equal rights, and I think that's one of them."

"I try to be tolerant of everyone, even people from Alabama," she told U.S. News and World Report.

She was a churchgoing, Christian. "But I do a lot of things the ladies of the church think I shouldn't do," she said in her 1977 book "Miss Lillian and Friends," as told to Beth Tartan and Rudy Hayes. "I smoke when I want to. I take a drink late in the evening." Bourbon was her favorite.

FIGURE 36: LILLIAN CARTER

Bessie Lillian Gordy was born in 1898 in Richland, Ga. She was a distant relative of Motown Records founder Berry Gordy. In 1921, the family moved to the tiny town of Plains, Ga., where Lillian became a registered nurse. In 1923, she married James Earl Carter, a successful farmer, who maintained a farm at their home in Archery, Ga., and a peanut farm in Plains three miles away. In racially segregated Georgia, Lillian supported integration, unlike just about every other White person in her community, including her husband. "She was the only person in Plains who would take up for Abraham Lincoln if he was ever brought up," said former first lady Rosalynn Carter, who grew up in Plains  Lillian became a Brooklyn Dodgers fan in 1947 when the team fielded the first Black player in the Major Leagues, Jackie Robinson of Cairo, Ga., and stayed a lifelong fan after the Dodgers moved to Los Angeles. "My mother watched or listened to every Dodgers game possible," Jimmy Carter wrote in his 2008 book "A Remarkable Mother." "She would call Tommy Lasorda to complain about managerial decisions he had made."

While working as a nurse, Lillian raised her four children: James Jr. (Jimmy), Gloria, Ruth and Billy. When James Sr. died in 1953, Jimmy resigned as a Navy nuclear submarine officer and moved to Plains to take over the family farming business. In 1956, Lillian became housemother at the Kappa Alpha fraternity at Auburn University in Auburn, Ala., where she was known as "Miss Lilly." At the 1964 Democratic convention, she was a delegate for President Lyndon B. Johnson.

Jimmy, meanwhile, followed his father's footsteps into state politics, winning election to the state Senate in 1962. (James Sr., a conservative Democrat and segregationist, had been elected to the Georgia House of Representatives a year before his death.)

In late 1966, it was Lillian who made headlines. "Mrs. Lillian Carter, the 68-year-old mother of State Sen. Jimmy Carter, leaves Tuesday for a two-year tour of duty with the Peace Corps in India," United Press International reported.

Lillian said she got the idea while watching "The Tonight Show Starring Jack Paar" and saw a Peace Corps promotion with the words: "Age Is No Barrier." In India, she worked in a one-room clinic providing family planning for poor couples and treating people with leprosy.

Later, after her son became Georgia governor, Lillian recalled that while staying in the governor's mansion one night, "Jimmy came in and said, 'Mama, I'm going to run for president.' I was so startled I said president of what?"

Carter was a dark-horse Democratic candidate in the 1976 presidential race. "Miss Lillian" sat in a rocking chair in Plains and greeted visiting journalists, Carter biographer Douglas Brinkley recounted in the PBS film "Jimmy Carter."

"Welcome to Plains! It's so nice to see you! Would you like some lemonade?" she would say. When a New York reporter pressed her about her son's claim of never telling a lie, Lillian conceded he tells "white lies." When the reporter pushed her to define "white lies," Miss Lillian said, "Remember when I said, 'Welcome to Plains, and how good it is to see you'? That's a white lie."

She had a hard time telling even white lies. That summer, actor Robert Redford came to Plains for dinner with the Carter family. As reporters waited outside the house, "Lillian Carter stuck her head out the door," the Atlanta Constitution reported. "'I wish it was Paul Newman,' she called.

After Carter defeated Republican incumbent Gerald Ford, Lillian soon was charming the press in Washington. She became a diplomatic asset. In 1977, she made an emotional return to India to represent the United States at the funeral of India's president and visited the clinic outside Bombay where she had worked in the Peace Corps. She was "mobbed" by 4,000 residents who sang a song about "Nurse Lillian," the Associated Press reported.

In 1978, columnist Jack Anderson revealed a confidential State Department report on her visit to Italy's new president Alessandro Pertini, a critic of U.S. foreign policy. "It is clear that Pertini was completely won over by Mrs. Carter's personal manner and by the purpose of her trip," Anderson wrote.

Lillian Carter died of breast cancer on Oct. 30, 1983, at age 85. In 1986, the Peace Corps established the Lillian Carter Award, recognizing exceptional volunteers who served at age 50 or older. In 2001, Jimmy Carter dedicated a nursing center in her honor in Plains.

He told NPR's Michel Martin in 2008: "I think my mother's life personifies, better than anybody I know, what America ought to be. She believed in peace, humility, service of others, human rights, forgiveness ... she was strong-willed but still adhering to the basic moral values that make America a great nation."

# CHAPTER 35

# ART BUCHWALD: EXIT LAUGHING

By Ronald G. Shafer
(A personal remembrance)

Visiting humor writer Art Buchwald in hospice in early 2006 was like being on "The Tonight Show." One morning when I was sitting next to him the mother of Jordan's Queen Noor walked in. I got up, gave her my chair and moved to a nearby couch. Meanwhile, Art was laughing on the phone with Larry Gelbart, the creator of the TV show "M*A*S* H."

"I love it here," Buchwald wrote about his hospice experience. "I hold court in the big living room. We sit for hours talking about the past, and since it's my show, we talk about anything that comes to my mind."

At age 80, suffering from kidney disease, Buchwald was relying on hospice care just as former President Jimmy Carter did after he entered home hospice care in Georgia at 98 in 2023 and former First Lady Rosalynn Carter did before dying at 96. The Carters faced death with dignity and with acclaim for their lifetime contributions to the world. In his final days, Buchwald made hospice and humor models for living life to the end.

In his heyday, the elf-like Buchwald who wore big horn-rim glasses was famed for a humor column poking fun at Washington. The column first caused a storm, he boasted, when he claimed FBI chief J. Edgar Hoover was "a mythical person thought up by Reader's Digest." In 1982 he won the Pulitzer Prize for commentary.

A stroke slowed the humorist in 2000 but he limped on. The next year as a Wall Street Journal editor I invited him to be my guest at the White House Correspondents' dinner. (We had been friends since I wrote about him in 1969). He held onto my arm for balance as he walked through the hotel grinning to the cheers of his news colleagues. At dinner, the widower even hit on a young female Journal reporter, Jackie Calmes, who let him down gently with, "Why Mr. Buchwald. My mother is a big fan of yours."

FIGURE 37: ART BUCHWALD

Then in 2006, Buchwald suffered kidney and vascular problems. Doctors amputated one of his legs just below the knee. He refused dialysis, and in February went into the Washington Home and Community Hospices, which he described as "a place where you go when you want to go." But he continued to write.

"When you are in a hospice, you get a chance to sleep a lot," he wrote. "I have this recurring dream. I am at Dulles airport and I have a reservation to go to heaven." He wrote that he was all the way to the departure gate when a loudspeaker announced: "Because of inclement weather, the flight to heaven has been canceled today. You can come back tomorrow, and we'll put you on standby."

Then a funny thing had started happening. Buchwald's kidneys began getting better. "I am writing this article from a hospice," he wrote. "But being in the hospice didn't work out exactly the way I wanted it to. By all rights I should have finished my time here five or six weeks ago -- at least that's all Medicare would pay for."

In July, he left hospice for his summer home. "Instead of going straight upstairs, I am going to Martha's Vineyard," he wrote. He joked about death: "My ashes are going to be spilled over every Trump building in New York." In November, he even published a final book, "Too Soon To Die." He returned to Washington to promote the book. He was hilarious when I saw him speak to an audience at one auditorium, but at the end he broke down in tears while urging his listeners to remember to be kind to others.

He kept his sense of humor as he was dying of kidney failure at 81 on Jan. 17, 2007 at his son's home in Washington, the Washington Post reported. His longtime buddy Post Vice President-at-Large Benjamin C. Bradlee said Buchwald, joking about his obituary getting top public attention, told friends, "I just don't want to die the same day Castro does." (Cuba's Fidel Castro was seriously ill at the time but didn't die until 2016 at 90.)

Buchwald was determined to exit laughing. The day after his death the New York Times ran an on-line video he had recorded the previous summer. It showed him grinning into the camera and saying, "Hi, I'm Art Buchwald, and I just died."

He still wasn't finished. He also had arranged a memorial at the Kennedy Center in Washington, D.C. for hundreds of friends who received a bookmark invitation that read, "The hottest ticket in town." Seats in the Eisenhower Theater were assigned. I sat next to JFK speechwriter Ted Sorenson on my left and astronaut John Glenn on my right.

Humor columnist Dave Barry and NBC-TV newsman Tom Brokaw hosted the Buchwald memorial. Barry said of his old friend, "He talked funny, he wrote funny and damned if he didn't figure out a way to die funny."

# OTHER BOOKS
# BY RONALD G. SHAFER

Breaking News All Over Again; The History Behind Today's Headlines. Amazon.com

When The Dodgers Were Bridegrooms. Gunner McGunnigle And the Back To Back Pennants of the 1889 and 1890 Brooklyn Bridegrooms. McFarland Publishing

The Carnival Campaign. How The Rollicking 1840 Campaign Of Tippecanoe and Tyler Too Changed Presidential Elections Forever, Chicago Review Press

Minor Memos, The Wacky Side of Politics and Power from The Wall Street Journal's Washington Wire Column, Andrews-McMeel

The Complete Book of Home Buying with Michael Sumichrast, Dow Jones Books

The New Complete Book of Home Buying with Michael Sumichrast, McGraw-Hill

How To Get Your Car Repaired Without Getting Gypped with Margaret Bresnahan Carlson, Simon & Shuster

www.ingramcontent.com/pod-product-compliance
Lightning Source LLC
Chambersburg PA
CBHW081546250726
48653CB00009B/3300